The Little Darlings

Also by Mary Cable

Dream Castles

American Manners and Morals
  with the editors of American Heritage

Black Odyssey: The Case of the Slaveship Amistad

The Avenue of the Presidents

El Escorial
  with the editors of Newsweek Books

The Little Darlings:

A History of Child Rearing
in America

MARY CABLE

Charles Scribner's Sons
New York

Copyright © 1972, 1974, 1975 Mary Cable

Library of Congress Cataloging in Publication Data

Cable, Mary.
  The little darlings.

    1. Children—Management—History.   2. Children in
the United States—History.   I. Title.
HQ769.C25   649'.1'0973   75–1025
ISBN 0–684–14219–8

This book published simultaneously in the
United States of America and in Canada—
Copyright under the Berne Convention

Two selections "S*x Education" and "Bringing Up Baby"
appeared in slightly different form in AMERICAN HERITAGE.

1 3 5 7 9 11 13 15 17 19 C/C 20 18 16 14 12 10 8 6 4 2

Printed in the United States of America

For Cassandra, with love

Acknowledgments

First, I want to express my gratitude to Dr. Milton J. E. Senn for allowing me to quote from the interviews compiled by him in his Oral Histories of the Child Development Movement in the United States (on file at the National Library of Medicine, Bethesda, Maryland). Thanks are also due to the very helpful and dedicated librarians of the Child Study Association, the Rare Book Rooms of the New York Public Library and the Library of Congress, and the American Psychiatric Association, Washington, D.C.

Grateful acknowledgment is made to the following publishers for permission to quote from works published by them: J. B. Lippincott Company, for quotations from *Henry James: The Untried Years 1843–1870*, by Leon Edel (copyright 1953 by Leon Edel); and from *Nancy Shippen, Her Journal Book*, compiled and edited by Ethel Armes (copyright 1935 by Ethel Armes); to Houghton Mifflin Company for a passage from *A Diary from Dixie*, by Mary Boykin Chesnut, edited by Ben Ames Williams; to William Morrow and Company, Inc., for permission to quote from *Blackberry Winter*, by Margaret Mead (copyright © 1972 by Margaret Mead); to The University Press of Virginia for quotations from *The Journal and Letters of Philip Vickers Fithian*, edited by Hunter Dickinson Farish; to Henry Regnery for a verse of the poem "Father and Son" by Edgar A. Guest; to the Harvard University Press for sentences from a letter of Abigail Adams; and to Doubleday and Company for a passage from *Culture and Commitment: A Study of the Generation Gap*, by Margaret Mead (copyright © 1970 by Margaret Mead).

Foreword

"HOW SHALL WE ORDER THE CHILD AND WHAT SHALL WE DO UNTO him?" According to the Bible, Samson's parents put this question to an Angel of the Lord and received the surprising reply, "Never cut his hair." This was surely an odd piece of advice, but perhaps no more odd than many other bits of how-to lore that parents have been offered through the centuries. "How shall we order the child?" is an age-old, often frantic question. When he misbehaves, shall we hit him, and, if so, how hard? When he cries, shall we soothe him or leave him screaming in his cradle? Will he thrive on a diet of ale and pork pie? And, if not, shall we dose him with opium? Or with minced snails and earthworms, boiled in rhubarb water?

Since the days of the first colonists, American children have consistently startled and not infrequently dismayed their elders. In 1657, in the Massachusetts Bay Colony, the Reverend Eleazar Rogers wrote to a friend in England, "I find the greatest trouble and grief about the rising generation. . . . Much ado I have with my own family . . . the young breed doth much aflict me. . . ."

Ever since that first generation, there has been recurring evidence that children of the New World are somehow different from and harder to handle than their counterparts east of the Atlantic. Various causes have been suggested: the climate, the diet, the water, the shape of American heads, and the possibility that Satan is running North America. Parents, always with the greatest conscientiousness and concern, have run the gamut of child-rearing methods, from birch rod to lollipop. In the Puritan view, a child was born evil and had to be beaten, lectured, and continually catechized in order to give him a chance of salvation. From this rigid tenet, the climate of child care changed, slowly and unevenly, until by the mid-nineteenth century the prevailing attitude was that an infant was neither good nor bad, but a characterless nothing, a tabula rasa; and that it was his nurture, not his nature, that would make him good or evil. In our century we went further, until the newborn was credited with every potential goodness and virtue, which the inept, heavy-handed, wretched parents were more than likely to destroy.

With a view to separating the truth from legend, this book proposes to trace the history of American ways with children. For the most part, these will be middle-class, mainstream ways —for to try to cover every ethnic, class, racial, and religious variation would mean a book of almost unmanageable length and complexity.

Within this framework, we will see how, through the generations, our children have been father to the man and mother to the woman, and why they have so often seemed different from their Old World cousins.

In the course of it all, perhaps we will discover new insights about ourselves.

Contents

ix

Illustrations

PART ONE

The Colonies

A Puritan girl: Alice Mason
The Adams National Historic Site, National Park Service
Department of the Interior

THE SEVENTEENTH CENTURY

Upon a World Vain, Toylsom, Foul,
A journey now ye enter.
The welfare of your living Soul
You dangerously adventure.

SO BEGINS *YOUTH'S DIVINE PASTIME*, A SEVENTEENTH-CENTURY volume intended for the light entertainment of young Puritans. For the children of the first American colonists, the journey between birth and adulthood was as perilous and uncharted as a voyage on the North Atlantic—and even rougher, judging by the fact that about half the little travelers died before they reached the age of ten. Yet in spite of this great mortality, the colonies were teeming with young people, for the average life expectancy was thirty-two, and nearly half the population was under twenty. (In 1970, 20 percent of the population was under twenty.) However, society was no more child-oriented than armies of the time were oriented toward privates. A seventeenth-century child, like a seventeenth-century private, had neither voice nor rights

3

and he was under the complete control of a supreme general—his father. According to the Puritan leader John Robinson, fathers, "by their greater wisdom and authority," were better suited than mothers for disciplining children. A mother's role was to bear, suckle, and care for infants, but after the first few months, fathers should take over and "by their severity" correct "the fruits of their mother's indulgence."

As far as physical care was concerned, colonial parents depended on advice handed down from earlier generations in the Old World. No sooner was an infant born than he found out what a Toylsom World he had got into: his mouth was swabbed out with a rough, unsanitary rag that was likely to scrape the skin from his tongue and toothless gums, and a stiff rod was laid against his back and neck, held rigidly in place by linen bands that wrapped him from chest to thighs (he was spared the neck-to-foot swaddling of continental babies). The rod was to keep his spine straight and his head from wobbling. While waiting for his mother's milk to start flowing, the baby might be plied with indigestible tidbits from the family table. Sometimes a considerate mother or nurse would chew these for him first. It was usual for colonial mothers of all classes to breast-feed their own children (unlike their English contemporaries), for wet nurses were not easily available. Efforts to bring up an infant "by hand" by offering him cow's milk in a pewter or leathern bottle were notoriously lethal. Anyway, parents feared that a child fed on the milk of a cow would grow up with a bovine temperament.

In the seventeenth century, nobody bathed much, and babies were bathed seldom or never to avoid their taking cold. They were kept as warm and airless as buns in the oven and were not infrequently suffocated under constricting covers or inadvertently squashed by mother or father while sharing the parental bed. One of the numerous, early-expiring children of Cotton Mather was "overlain" by its nurse. In many families, especially where soap and cloth were scarce, diapers were not washed after every use but were simply hung up to dry in front of the fire before being put back on. Since the safety pin was still some two hundred years in the future, diapers were secured by strings, buttons, and straight pins.

If the child sickened, which was likely, a physician might be called in, who would prescribe bleeding, purging, blistering, and dosing, just as he would for an adult. There was no special field of medicine called pediatrics, nor was there a seventeenth-century Dr. Spock to minister to the emotional growing pains of children or to advise parents regarding discipline. The lack was not felt, for child care was not the subject of intense interest that it is today, and childhood, as we think of it, did not exist. Children were considered to differ from men and women only in respect to size, experience, and capability. They were coaxed or bludgeoned into joining society more or less as if they were delinquent or dull-witted adults. Furthermore, they were expected to be grateful to their parents for giving them birth and apologetic for the trouble they caused by simply being children. The New England colonist Anne Bradstreet, who wrote poetry while raising eight children, put these sentiments into the mouth of a child in her poem "The Four Ages of Man," published in 1671:

> With tears into the world I did arrive.
> My mother still did waste as I did thrive,
> Who yet with love and all alacrity,
> Spending, was willing to be spent for me.
> With wayward cries I did disturb her rest,
> Who sought still to appease me with the breast:
> With weary arms she danc'd and ByBy sung,
> When wretched I ingrate had done the wrong. . . .

That children were hopelessly indebted to their parents was

taken for granted everywhere. It was not so much a religious tenet as a social one, handed down from time immemorial. The Puritans, however, differed from other people in having acquired, from John Calvin, a new point of view about child rearing: parents must educate and discipline their children in order to give them every chance for salvation. Those who failed in this responsibility would answer for it on Judgment Day. "The education of our children is a point of inexpressable consequence," Cotton Mather said. "Ruin families and you ruin all." (The word *education* in the seventeenth century meant not only reading and writing but all aspects of child care.)

For this reason, the Puritans were at once more severe with their children than members of other communions, and more concerned with each individual child. The traditional attitude toward babes-in-arms was that they were like live dolls, quite incapable of lasting impressions or ideas. But to Calvinists they were morsels of pure depravity. When they grew older and their labor was needed, Calvinists felt a holy zeal in putting them to work in order to save them from the sins of idleness. Apparently some parents took this duty so seriously that a restraining note was in order: John Cotton, one of the first New England clergymen, wrote of little children: ". . . their bodyes are too weak to labour, and their minds to study are too shallow . . . even the first seven years are spent in pastimes and God looks not much at it."

In most Puritan colonial families, however, seven-year-olds were already veteran workers. A Puritan infant, lying in its cradle shaking a rattle, was enjoying the only unearned and unguilt-ridden recreation of its lifetime. Toddlers were put to work feeding chickens, winding spools, gathering kindling, and the like. By the time a girl was six or seven, she could sew, knit, weave, and spin. At the same age, her brothers knew the principles of farming and were nearly ready to be apprenticed to whatever craft or trade they would pursue for the rest of their lives. For a child to play was not only anathema to most Puritan minds, it was a legal offense—at least, in the theocratic Massachusetts Bay Colony. According to an order of the Bay Government in 1641, "it is desired and will be expected that all masters of families should see that their children and servants should be industriously implied [employed] so as the mornings and evenings and other seasons may not bee lost as formerly they have bene." The following year, another order required that children and servants who watched cattle should at the same time "bee set to some other impliment withal, as spinning upon the rock [a hand-held spinning device], knitting, weveing tape, etc.; and that boyes and girles bee not suffered to converse together, so as may occasion any wanton, dishonest or immodest behavior. . . ."

What were they like, these hard-working, serious, conscience-driven children? For us, they must remain shadowy, for their elders wrote little about them, and only occasionally in such a way as to bring them to life, as when Judge Samuel Sewall writes in his diary, "Little Hull said Apple plainly"; or tells us that his small daughter Betty wept with fear at biblical stories about hellfire; or that another of his children threw a piece of brass and hit his sister.

But if we do not have many vivid descriptions of children, we at least know what their daily routine was. Families rose at "break-a-day," said their prayers, ate cornmeal porridge washed down with cider or small beer, and went promptly to their tasks. Dinner was served at noon, or earlier, a substantial meal of cornmeal pudding (likely to be served first, to take the edge off too-keen appetites), roast meat, bread, and "sauce," which was any kind of cooked vegetable or fruit. If there were not enough chairs or if the table was too small (the average New England household in the latter seventeenth century comprised nine persons), the children stood, with two eating out of one wooden trencher. Drinking cups and bottles were made of leather or pewter, and poorer families passed one cup around the table. Babies old enough to have been weaned sat in their mother's laps and shared in whatever was being served.

Children were expected to remain silent unless spoken to. Cotton Mather wrote in his diary, "I will have my table talk facetious as well as instructive . . . yett I will have the Exercise continually intermixed." (So, apparently, he allowed a touch of levity.) There were strict rules governing children's table manners, set forth in books of etiquette brought over from England and used in all the colonies: "Stuff not thy Mouth so as to fill thy Cheeks," "Blow not thy Meat," "Throw not anything under the Table," "Dip not thy Meat in the Sauce," "Take not salt with a greasy knife," "Smell not of thy Meat, nor put it to thy nose; turn it not the other Side upward to view it upon thy Plate," and "Foul not the Tablecloth."

In Massachusetts, a law passed in 1642 required that every village have a school. It was not always carried out, but if there were no school, children and servants were required to be catechized and taught the three Rs at home. If not, the head of the household was liable for a heavy fine. As a result, New England became the most literate part of seventeenth-century America.

When a Puritan child was neither working nor studying, he was apt to be saying his prayers. Grace was said before each meal and a thanksgiving after; there were family prayers every morning and evening, and everyone who was old enough to talk was supposed to address himself privately to the Almighty upon awakening and before going to sleep; all this in addition to six hours of sermons and psalms on Sundays and a religious lecture on Thursday evenings. Newborn babes were carried to meeting to be christened, even when the weather was cold enough to freeze the holy water. For young and old alike, no excuses were accepted, short of serious illness, for nonattendance at meeting. Boys and girls sat separately and were discouraged from playing or falling asleep by a tithing-man equipped with a stout staff.

Each Puritan day ended with a meal of porridge, perhaps accompanied by milk and fruit, and an early bedtime. There were almost no amusements especially devised for children, but some of the duties of the household and farm combined necessity with a cheerful get-together of family and neighbors: cornhusking, rat-killing, quilting, apple-paring, and the making of soap, sausage, or candles—to name a few. Weddings, ordinations, and funerals were all occasions for robust eating and drinking, from which no age was excluded. Training Day, when the militia was mustered, was the most lively occasion in the Puritan year—a holiday for everyone, with parades and prizes for marksmanship.

Valentine's Day was tolerated by the theocratic state, if reluctantly. As for dancing, although there were those who pointed out a biblical passage about pious people dancing before the Lord, most Puritans could not imagine a pious dancer. John Cotton condemned "lascivious dancing to wanton ditties, and in amorous gestures and wanton dalliances, especially after great feasts," and no proper Puritan child was sent to dancing school until well along in the eighteenth century. In fact, there were no dancing masters on New England soil until after the Bay Colony lost its charter in 1684 and became like any other English colony, with Church of England clergymen and a Royal Governor sent over from the mother country. On Christmas Day, the Anglicans feasted, while the Puritans made a great show of ignoring them and carrying on work and business as usual. Not until the nineteenth century was Christmas to become a joyful time for all children.

So important was proper child rearing in the eyes of Puritans that the state, through the medium of tithing-men, kept a big-brotherish eye on every household. In Boston, for example, a tithing-man checked up regularly on the behavior of ten families assigned to him. To a child with a guilty conscience he must have been a terrifying sight, a kind of personification of a vengeful God, as he approached inexorably down the street and thumped the doorknocker. As every child well knew, Calvin had said, "Those who violate the parental authority by contempt or rebellion are not men but monsters. Therefore the Lord commands all those who are disobedient to their parents to be put to death." No one in New England ever saw this fearful dictum actually carried out, but Connecticut had a law on the books that called for death to all disobedient young people over the age of fourteen. In all the New England colonies, insubordinate children and servants (who were often children) could be—and sometimes were—sentenced to a public whipping. More often they were forced to make a public confession at meeting, or were made the specific target of a denunciatory sermon. Or they might be assigned a stint of appropriate reading, such as Cotton Mather's *The Family Well Ordered or An Essay to Render Parents and Children Happy in One Another* (1699). "Children," Mather wrote, "If by Undutifulness to your Parents, you incur the Curse of God, it won't be long before you go down into Obscure Darkness, even, into Utter Darkness; God has Reserv'd for you the Blackness of Darkness forever." And an even worse fate awaited Undutiful Parents.

Some of the Puritan theories of child rearing were first set forth by John Robinson, patriarch of the *Mayflower* pilgrims. Robinson had stayed behind in Holland when the *Mayflower*

Mrs. Elizabeth Freake and her baby Mary
Worcester Art Museum, Worcester, Massachusetts

sailed in 1620, but his admonitions and writings went with the Pilgrims and were treasured by them. His *Of Children and Their Education* seems more imaginative than the works of Cotton Mather on the same subject, perhaps because Robinson lived at a time (from 1575 to 1625) when Puritanism was a growing, dynamic institution, whereas Mather lived after the peak was passed and was constantly shoring up rather than building.

Children, Robinson said, are "a blessing great but dangerous." Besides the danger inherent in birth, sickness, and youthful recklessness, they are subject to many spiritual dangers, "nourishing and increasing the corruption which they bring into the world with them." And he quoted Proverbs 22:15: "Foolishness is bound up in the heart of a child, which the rod of correction must drive out." He recommended that the rod be employed early, even before the child is aware of himself vis-à-vis the world. "Children should not know, if it could be kept from them, that they have a will. . . ." He thought a child ought never to be heard to say "I will" or "I will not," except in assent. He assured parents that a child without a will would not grow up "abject" and "unapt to great employments"—though he did not explain how to bring this about.

It was important, he thought, that children should go to school early and find a calling "rather under than above their estate." Parents do not see their children clearly—"the crow thinks her own bird fairest"—and sometimes cause their children to fall "Icaruslike, in a sea of mischief and misery, by their flying too high a pitch." Before undertaking any calling, a young person must show an aptitude for it: "the midwife . . . cannot make the woman to be delivered that was not first with child." Despite his belief that children must be severely disciplined, Robinson was ahead of his time in recognizing that children must be permitted a certain amount of childishness. "Fruits ripened by art before their time are neither toothsome nor wholesome; so children made men when they should be children prove children when they should be men."

John Robinson exemplified the sturdy nonconformist, who could not compromise with life as he found it in England. Although he never crossed the Atlantic, he was typical of those who did: a stubborn, individualistic, shrewd, ingenious, and able English yeoman, whose traits were later to be considered typical of the Yankee. Since these traits also offer a clue to the distinctive character and behavior of the American child (through the centuries called precocious by some and brattish by others), it is worth our while to examine them.

The yeomen of England were an impressive lot. For centuries they had been protecting their rights against the gentry and the nobility and it had made them feisty, aloof, and hard to budge. It was logical that the uncompromising religion of Calvin should have appealed to many of them. The very fact that the upper classes embraced the Anglican church was almost enough in itself to alienate the yeomen. Furthermore, being hard workers by tradition, they liked the high value that the Calvinist faith placed on work, thrift, and practicality. Gentlemen, living on the income of landed estates, considered work beneath them. Yeomen had always been obliged to work, and now, as Puritans, they felt that they were doing something pleasing to the Lord. They liked the word *calling*, as a synonym for *occupation*. It meant that they had been called by a divine voice to whatever their work was, even if it was lowly. If, when a boy reached the age of apprenticeship, he was unable to hear what the divine voice was telling him, his parents listened for him. "We are bringing up children for God," John Robinson wrote, adding, from Ephesians 6:4, "He trusts us with the bringing them up for him; in his nurture and instruction."

The Puritans delighted in pointing to a scriptural justification for everything they did, and obviously, in order to do this really well—to study the Bible through and through and ponder its nuances and take notes at sermons—one had to be literate. And there was an even more important reason for literacy: according to Calvin, salvation was to be found through reading the scriptures. Thus, since every child was corrupted by original sin and in dire need of salvation, it behooved parents to teach him to read as soon as possible.

This requirement suited yeomen very well. Since medieval times they had valued literacy as a defense against untrustworthy lawyers, business rivals, and aristocrats. Some had taught their wives and children to read and work sums so that they could take produce to market and avoid being cheated. At Oxford and Cambridge, the largest single segment of English society among the student body came from the yeoman class (before the Restoration). Although yeomen had little to do with the government of England on a national or international level, 75 percent of the country was governed from villages and it was the yeomen who filled such posts as mayor, alderman, and sheriff. The Lord Mayor of London was traditionally of this class. The famous Dick Whittington was exceptional in rising as fast as he did, but it was common for the important men of London to be the sons or grandsons of country yeomen.

When Calvinism reached England, yeomen welcomed a religious reason for doing what they were anxious to do anyway. Elizabethan Puritans, such as John Robinson, taught their children to read and forbade them to associate with non-Puritans. Being persecuted under King James I, Robinson and a group of his coreligionists in southeast England ran away to live in Holland. But it was not far enough. William Bradford, who was one of the group and who later became governor of Plymouth Plantation, complained that the children of English Puritans were picking up unfortunate habits in Holland—

"drawn away by evill examples into extravagant and dangerous courses, getting ye raines off their necks and departing from their parents." The fugitives crossed the ocean and settled Plymouth. A few years later, John Winthrop and his followers settled the Massachusetts Bay Colony.

The Pilgrims were a humble group, including among them a number of artisans and ordinary laborers, while some of the people of the Bay were gentlemen's sons. The Pilgrims were Separatists, while the Bay Puritans wanted reform within the established Anglican church. Nevertheless, the two colonies managed to survive side by side and even learned to cooperate.

Certainly it would seem that both these theocratic states had a unique chance of making whatever they wished of their children. "Train up a child in the way he should go; and when he is old he will not depart from it" was one of the most frequently quoted verses in the Bible. But the trouble was that not only Puritans but many other sorts of people wanted to immigrate to New England, and not only was there no way of keeping them out, but some of them, those who were skilled artisans, were sorely needed. In midcentury, Cromwell shipped over hundreds of Scottish and Irish prisoners taken in battle, to be bound out as servants. There were also a few Huguenots and German Protestants, and a generous sprinkling of ne'er-do-wells of various nationalities, seeking to improve their lots in this world but with little interest in the next. In that century, almost everyone professed some religious affiliation, but there were many in New England who were too absorbed in worldly matters to suit the Puritan hierarchy. "And by this means the cuntree became pestered with many unworthy persons," wrote Governor Bradford.

Everyone, unworthy or not, was supposed to follow the laws of the theocratic state and was subject to fines if he did not. For a time the state tried to stamp out such behavior as "riotous conduct," "light carriage," and the wearing of bright or elaborate clothing, but its prohibitions proved little more deterring than the laws of Prohibition nearly three centuries later. And the worst of it was that when the children of the ruling theocrats saw other children playing, dancing, singing, and laughing, some of them hankered to do likewise and "get the raines off their necks."

"Generation gap" is a phrase coined in this century, but New England's founding fathers would have recognized its meaning. Their children, born in America or perhaps brought over as infants, were simply not zealous enough about religion. "It is a tough work, a wonderful hard matter to be saved," said the Reverend Thomas Shepard, addressing the young. Shepard was a noted preacher, of whom it was said that whenever he mounted the pulpit and delivered one of his hellfire sermons, "some or other of his Congregation were struck with great distress of Soul and cried in Agony." But in spite of his efforts, children and young people were not coming in to report that they had had the necessary spiritual "Experience" and were ready to join the church.

According to orthodox Calvinism, the only way to join the church was to undergo The Experience, which consisted of five specific and invariable steps. It could happen at any age. Sometimes children as young as six or seven reported that they had taken all five steps. First, one had to realize one's depraved condition and truly understand that, without salvation, one was inevitably headed for hell. Second, feeling utterly helpless, one must accept the will of God, no matter what that might be. ("If he save me, I shall be happy forever; if he damn me, I must justifie him," wrote Cotton Mather's brother Nathaniel, when, at the age of thirteen, The Experience overtook him.) The next step was a deep sense of peace and joy and a lively hope—but not a certainty—of salvation. Fourth came a public confession of one's sins and, fifth, the formal act of joining the church. Puritans did not believe in showing emotion, but they made an exception in this matter. Tears, groans, screams, grinding of teeth, and writhing on the floor—all were acceptable; indeed, they were expected.

"Early piety" was much admired in children. Among the few seventeenth-century books written especially for the young was *A Token for Children, Being an exact Account of the Conversion, Holy and Exemplary Lives, and Joyful Deaths of Several Young Children.* The work of a nonconformist English divine named James Janeway, the book first appeared in London in 1671 and was reprinted many times on both sides of the Atlantic for over a hundred years. It was just the sort of thing to please Cotton Mather, and he wrote an addition to it, *A Token for the Children of New England, Or, Some Examples of Children, in whome the Fear of God was Remarkably Budding before they Died, in several Parts of New-England, Preserved for the Encouragement of Piety in other Children.* All the stories end in painful illness and death, the only variation being that some of the children were never bad while others repented their tiny sins in time and joined their saintlier brethren in self-satisfied anticipation of heaven. Books like these seem to us excruciatingly morbid as well as tiresomely repetitious. But there must have been a different idea of what was morbid in a world where half the children died.

Another of Cotton Mather's books for the young was *Early Piety—Exemplified in the life and Death of Mr. Nathaniel Mather.* Nathaniel was a younger brother of Cotton, born in Boston in 1681. Although "secret prayer became very betimes one of his infant exercises," he was tortured by the fear that he would not be saved. At the age of thirteen he began to keep a diary and filled it with anxious passages. "What shall I do? What shall I do to be saved? Without a Christ I am undone, undone forevermore!

O Lord, let me have a Christ, though I lie in the mire for ever! O for a Christ! O for a Christ! a Christ! Lord give me a Christ or I die!" He confesses that he is "by nature a son of hell," and that "of myself I am helpless and undone, and without righteousness." (This was step two of the five steps to salvation.)

Nathaniel's fervor led him to organize Friday evening prayer meetings among other teen-agers—who must have been dedicated Puritans indeed, considering all the other praying they did during the week. Their object was to obtain from God "the success of the work of grace in New England, especially in Boston, on the souls of the rising generation." But still, according to his brother, Nathaniel was obsessed with the idea of his own sinfulness. His thoughts seemed to him blasphemous and vile and he had "a restless, raging agony in his mind." He wrote in his diary, "When very young I went astray from God. . . . Of the manifold sins which then I was guilty of, none so sticks upon me, as that being very young I was *whitling* on the Sabbath-day; and for fear of being seen, I did it behind the door. A great reproach of God! a specimen of that *atheism* that I brought into the world with me!"

The young man entered Harvard at the age of twelve and graduated at sixteen, and was working for a second degree when he died, not yet twenty. "Study killed him," wrote his brother, adding sadly, "One might suppose that such a 'walk with God' . . . should end in raptures and exstasies of assurance; but I am to tell you that this young person had them not." Puritans were conditioned never to count on a happy ending.

Was Nathaniel Mather a typical child of the Puritans? Surely he must have been an extreme case, but still, any child who is called an abominable and guilty sinner or a despicable worm or a fountain of sin on a regular basis is more than likely to become sober, cautious, and apprehensive at best, and, at worst, a raving paranoid. No wonder that Yankees dug into their work with such vigor, for every idle moment filled them with guilt and anxiety.

The Puritans were nothing if not forthright toward their children. They never avoided or sugarcoated any hard fact, preferring to "wrestle" with it; and of all hard facts, death was the hardest and most inescapable. By the time a colonial child reached his teens he had probably been to dozens of funerals and had watched by more than one deathbed in his own household. He had probably also read Janeway's *Deaths of Pious Children* and listened to special "children's sermons" filled with tidings of doom. Instead of the rhymes of Mother Goose (who did not come along until the eighteenth century), small Puritans were taught to recite:

> I in the Burying Place may see
> Graves shorter than I
> From Death's Arrest no Age is Free
> Young Children too may die;
> My God, may such an awful Sight
> Awakening be to me!
> Oh! that by Grace I might
> For Death prepared be.

The Book of Martyrs, while not written for children, was handed them as soon as they could read. The frontispiece was a woodcut showing a Protestant martyr, during the reign of Bloody Mary, going up in flames at the stake, while his wife and numerous children stand by. The notion of shielding the young from knowledge of violence, wickedness, or sex would have astonished a Puritan parent, who reasoned that the more they heard about such things, the better; it would make them consider their own wickedness and try to correct it. One of the most popular books for all ages—and one of the few produced in seventeenth-century America—was the narrative poem "The Day of Doom," by a Bay Colony minister, Michael Wigglesworth. Wigglesworth was not much of a poet, but he had a unique talent for conjuring up visions of horror and couching them in a hypnotic kind of doggerel. Especially designed to give children nightmares was the two-hundredth verse, which warned that a graceless child, before being tossed into the eternal flames, would be disowned by his mother, while his "pious father" would "rejoyce to hear Christ's voice adjudging him to pain."

Children who had seen infant brothers and sisters consigned to those short graves in the cemetery may have been comforted to learn from Wigglesworth that God reserves for infants "the easiest room in Hell." But to Hell they would certainly go, according to the doctrine of infant damnation. Mistress Anne Bradstreet stated the doctrine in one of her poems, describing a small child:

> Stained from birth with Adam's sinfull fact
> Thence I began to sin as soon as act:
> A perverse will, a love to what's forbid,
> A serpent's sting in pleasing face lay hid;
> A lying tongue as soon as it could speak,
> And fifth commandment do daily break.
> Oft stubborn, peevish, sullen, pout, and cry,
> Then naught can please and yet I know not why.

Unhappy children in colonial times had one advantage over modern ones: they became adults much sooner. Anne Bradstreet was married at fifteen and John Winthrop at seventeen without being considered precocious. One of Winthrop's sons was named his executor at fourteen. At eighteen, Samuel Sewall's father-in-law, John Hull, was an established gold- and silversmith. The undergraduates at Harvard were usually between twelve and sixteen. There was no segment of society called teen-agers—the very word was not invented until this century. Nor was there an "age of innocence," nor a sentimental feeling that there ought to be one. *Youth's Divine Pastime*, which was popular with colonial children for about a hundred years, offered a jaunty retelling of some of the most violent and erotic stories in the Bible. For example, here is:

LOT AND HIS TWO DAUGHTERS

When Sodom and Gommorah were
Consum'd by Fire that fell
From Heaven, and all that pleasant Land
Seem'd to resemble Hell;

Lot's daughters, thinking all Mankind
Had been destroy'd thereby
Contrive together how they may
Preserve Posterity.

They make their Father drunk with Wine
And then both with him lye
He being ignorant of this
Their wanton policy.

Thus Lot, whose righteous Soul was vext
With Sodom's wickedness,
And who to them a Preacher was
Of truth and righteousness,

Yet when his Daughters tempted him
To drink Wine to excess
He fell into that odious Vice
And Crime of Drunkenness,

Which caused him likewise to commit
That great and heinous Sin
Of incest with his Daughters, who
Were both with Child by him.

Great God! if such a Man as Lot
Was subject thus to fall
How right we daily upon thee
For Grace and Strength to call.

This nursery favorite was illustrated with a woodcut showing Lot sprawling boozily on a couch while his naked daughters
ply him with wine. Another lively illustration, accompanying a
poem called "The Levite and His Concubine," portrays the
Levite chopping his concubine into twelve pieces, she having just
been raped by a company of Sodomites, who (says the poem)
would really have preferred to enjoy the Levite himself.

The fact that *Youth's Divine Pastime* went into many editions
and beguiled four generations of children seems to answer any
questions we may have had about sex education among the
Puritans. There were no secrets from the young. However,
children and grown-ups alike were admonished to remember
that sex was the cause of Adam's downfall and was a reprehensi-
ble business, even in wedlock. Anne Bradstreet's poem "Childhood" begins,

> Ah me! conceived in sin and born with sorrow,
> A nothing, here today and gone tomorrow,
> Whose mean beginning blushing can't reveal
> But night and darkness must with shame conceal . . .

Works like this and "Lot and His Daughters" were put into
the hands of children because they showed how sex got people
into trouble. The Restoration poets, writing in England at about
the same time, found no audience in New England; they made
sex sound like fun, whereas, as every good Puritan knew, it was a
shameful, deplorable activity whose consequence was a lump of
corruption called a baby.

We have dwelt at such length on New England children
because the Puritan ethic has been the dominant one in our
country, and those earnest Puritan little ones, reciting their
catechisms or tending cattle and spinning at the same time, have

cast a long shadow. Thousands of New Englanders were among the pioneers of the West, bringing with them the Puritan ethic of hard work, self-sufficiency, and self-righteousness. And that ethic has persisted, even among people who have never set foot in a Calvinist meetinghouse. The Quakers of seventeenth-century Philadelphia placed as stern and strong an emphasis on religion as the Puritans did—though the two groups despised one another. But in the other middle colonies and in the southern ones, child-rearing customs were somewhat different, and, therefore, ought to be looked at separately.

The Dutch settlers on Manhattan and Long Island and up the Hudson River were followers of Calvin but, unlike their New England neighbors, they had not come to the New World in search of religious freedom. That they had at home. They came with the simple worldly desire to better themselves. Dutch ways with children were traditionally rather permissive—as the Pilgrims had so disapprovingly observed during their stay in Holland. Under the pioneer conditions of a new colony they became even more so. There was less emphasis on schools than in New England. What schools there were were coeducational, with the result that Dutch women were accustomed from childhood to being out in the world. More emancipated than the English, they might buy or inherit real estate. (This was unheard of in the English colonies; Connecticut was the first state to permit it, in 1809, followed by Ohio in 1835.) Women might also operate stores and businesses, which was exceptional among the English.

Still, Dutch children heard a great deal about hellfire and damnation and were catechized, just as in New England. And like all seventeenth-century people, they were taught to believe in witchcraft. Here are some questions and answers from a Dutch child's catechism:

Question: What is the second capital sin?
Answer: Witchcraft.

23

Question: Does Witchcraft appear in God's word?
Answer: Yes.
Question: Prove it.
Answer: [The respondent cites several biblical references.]
Question: Are there any people who say that there is no witchcraft?
Answer: The Sadducees of this day and the Libertines amongst the so-called Christians, who believe that all that is said of Satan and his workers are fables and that everything that takes place is perfectly natural.

Possibly because the Dutch colonists were so preoccupied with advancing themselves that they had no time for witch-hunts, no witches were ever executed in New Amsterdam, nor were there any hysterical children precipitating a witch-hunt, as happened in Salem.

New Amsterdam was annexed by the English in 1667. Its name was changed to New York, an English governor arrived, and English settlers—mostly Anglicans—poured in. But for many years it was very much like a Dutch town. The new rulers permitted Dutch to be taught in the schools and to be spoken as a first language in Dutch families. Only after 1776 were the latter required by law to learn English. The Dutch had several holidays that traditionally provided special fun for children, and the English were happy to take them over. Christmas had always been a time of general merriment in England, although not especially for children. The Dutch celebrated Saint Nicholas's Day, December 5, when that saint (also known as Sinter Klaas or Sancte Claus) brought presents for good children and a switch for bad ones; and January 6, Epiphany, when children in the street played a game of jumping over candles, and young boys, dressed as the three kings, went about the houses and taverns, getting free good cheer. The latter holiday has died out in America, but Saint Nicholas gradually began to visit New York children of all nationalities, not on December 5 but on Christmas

Eve (arriving via the chimney, as he did in Dutch houses); and now he seems to get around to all fifty states.

New Year's was another holiday enthusiastically celebrated by Dutch children, who got up early to blow horns and whistles and ring bells, while their elders paid calls and drank; so was Shrove Tuesday—the occasion of a children's masquerade; also May Day, Whitsuntide, and Saint Martin's Eve. To these the English added their own special holiday, Guy Fawkes' Day, loved by children because of its fireworks. There was an annual fair in New York toward the end of October, which brought toy booths, puppet shows, and plays. The Dutch Calvinists drew the line at dancing, but the English, being Anglicans, did not, and by 1700 New York children and young people had a wide choice of dancing classes. The dancing masters came from among an influx of French Huguenot immigrants, who also supplied teachers of French, music, and embroidery, and established New York as a place where young ladies from other colonies were often sent to acquire these elegancies.

There were blue laws in New York, not as strict as Boston's, but strict enough to clearly distinguish Sunday from the rest of the week. A statute of 1673 decreed that if an officer of the law caught any children playing or making noise in the street on Sunday during church services, he was to confiscate their hats or jackets, to be redeemed by their parents on payment of a fine. Sunday dancing, cardplaying, or competitive sports were not allowed, but other pastimes were permitted that young people enjoyed—sleighing and skating in winter, promenading in summer, and kissing games anytime.

Virginia, Maryland, and South Carolina had more in common with New York than with New England or Pennsylvania. These four colonies were distinctive for their vast land grants, ruled over by gentlemen who had been lucky or conniving enough to accumulate land. Thousands of acres were thus controlled by one man, like self-sufficient little kingdoms. New York had more black slaves than the other northern colonies. The custom began, in wealthy families, of giving each small white child a small black child-slave as servant and companion. Still, before 1700, slavery was not a significant factor in any North American colony. In the South, as in the North, the great majority of families lived on small farms, and any servants they had were white, indentured ones.

Like New England children, those in the South came of an Anglo-Saxon culture, worked hard, grew up early, and were likely to die young. Not so many of them went to school—partly because the Anglican church to which most of them belonged did not equate salvation with education; partly because the Royal Governor and those who ruled Virginia did not believe in learning for the masses; and partly because there were few villages in the South, where schools might be supported.

There were a great many poor people in the southern colonies, and a great many unattached children and orphans. During the first decades of Virginia settlement, labor was badly needed there, and in 1619, the City of London sent one hundred indigent boys and girls picked up off the streets to be indentured servants. Some were unwilling to go, so the city petitioned for and received authority to send them anyway. According to the petition, these were children "of whom the city is especially desirous to be disburdened, and in Virginia under severe masters they may be brought to goodness." Besides those sent under official auspices, many children in England were "spirited" or kidnapped by ship captains or their agents, who were paid handsomely for them by colonists in need of servants and farm workers. Not as many family units immigrated to Virginia and Maryland as they did to New England, and single men who acquired land were in dire need of help. The practice of sending poor children to southern colonies continued for about fifty years, until most of the settlers had either slaves, bond-servants, or their own useful families of children.

Toward the end of the century, poor people who wanted to immigrate to the New World were likely to head for Pennsylvania. Many of these were Germans, the first sizable non-English group of immigrants, and many came as Redemptioners. This meant that in exchange for their passage, the captain of the ship they traveled in might sell them as bond-servants for a period of three to six years. It not infrequently happened that some members of an immigrant family died during the voyage, and the survivors had to redeem not only their own passage expenses but those of their deceased relatives. Sometimes child victims of this system became, in effect, slaves for life.

Rich or poor, north or south, American children were already developing a distinctive temperament. In a 1685 sermon, Cotton Mather remarked, "The Youth in this country are verie Sharp and early Ripe in their Capacities." The next century was to prove how right that terrifying old Puritan was.

Connecticut gentry: Mrs. Benjamin Tallmadge and her children
of the town of Litchfield
Courtesy of the Litchfield Historical Society

2

THE EIGHTEENTH CENTURY

DURING THE EARLY DAYS OF THE COLONIES, MOST FAMILIES were without many material comforts, but we must not infer from this that they had no class consciousness. Status depended on the social position they had brought with them from England. In Massachusetts, for example, everyone knew that the Winthrops were gentlefolk, even though they wore homespun and their children worked as hard as other children. That gentlefolk might work with their hands or in trade without losing caste was a major change from English custom and has persisted throughout our history, but it has never eliminated snobbery. No sooner were the colonial meetinghouses built than people were seated in their pews according to rank—the families of magistrates and ministers in the best pews and so on down to the Negro and Indian slaves, who occupied the back of the gallery. The "better sort"—including children—were addressed as Master and Mistress; below them, adults were called Goodman and Goodwife and their children went by their first names; and among the very humble, first names sufficed for all.

At Harvard and Yale, the boys were at first ranked according to scholastic achievement, but by the end of the seventeenth century, according to the prestige of their fathers' callings. Sons of ministers ranked first, followed by sons of magistrates, lawyers, merchants, shopkeepers, master mariners, physicians, schoolmasters, farmers, militia officers, artisans, seamen, and servants. Ministers' sons were the most numerous, since in New England there was one minister to every thirty-five families and their sons were the most likely to attend college. The first servant's son to attend Harvard graduated with the class of 1673. The superior-ranking boys got the best seats in the dining hall and classrooms, as well as the banister-side of staircases. This arrangement lasted nearly until the Revolution, with the refinements of precedence becoming ever more intricate. Yale switched to an alphabetical system in 1770 and Harvard a year later, after a furor over whether one boy's father had been a Justice of the Peace longer than another's. Upperclassmen had certain privileges over freshmen; one was that they were allowed to mingo (from *mingere*, Latin: to urinate) against the college wall, while the freshmen had to find another place.

After the pioneer years of colonial life, social rank inevitably came to be connected with material possessions. Puritan austerity notwithstanding, clothing was a mark of social status for young and old alike. In order to dress his family in finery of any kind, a Massachusetts man was legally required to have either a liberal education or an annual income of two hundred pounds—a law that was often disobeyed in spite of punishment by fines and in the stocks. In 1676, in Northampton, Massachusetts, a sixteen-year-old girl who had been arrested for wearing a hooped petticoat defiantly wore it to court. At that time the law also forbade boys and men to wear "long hair after the manner of ruffians and barbarous Indians contrary to God's word." But by 1700, long hair was accepted and it was wigs that were special anathema. Yet there were wigs even for little boys.

In the eighteenth century when many hardworking Puritans and Quakers became wealthy they did not hesitate to spend lavishly on clothes. At Harvard, in 1754, the students had to be admonished not to wear silk nightgowns. Children were dressed as much like grown-ups as possible and parents who could afford it put stays and hoops and long, stiff dresses on their little girls, and kneebritches, embroidered coats and vests, and lace-trimmed shirts on the boys. In 1739, the life of a *ten-year-old* New York girl was described as follows:

> Head-dresses, masks, necklaces, gloves, patches, fans, shoes, girdles, rings, with many other beguiling things;—all this while no manner of religion is going forward. The young lady's days are passed in receiving and paying visits; her nights at balls and masquerades, or at cards and dice. The father thinks to gain a rich husband by equipping her after a manner superior to her rank, and the mother for her part very willingly conceives the father's folly will one day tend to the child's good.

Fascinating new materials were now finding their way to the colonies—silks, gauzes, nankeen from Nanking, and calicoes from Calcutta. Even babies wore embroidered mitts, and little girls wore hoods, sunbonnets, or face masks, to protect their complexions. To illustrate the change in the lives of New England children of "the better sort," we have the delightful diary kept by eleven-year-old Anna Green Winslow in 1771. This little girl had been sent to Boston from Newfoundland to live with an aunt and partake of the city's educational and social advantages. In the Puritan tradition, she dutifully took notes on Sabbath-day sermons, recording a warning to young people that fine dress would never make them beautiful if their souls were unholy. As Nanny wrote it down, the minister had said, "You may think me very unpolite . . . but I must go a little further and tell you, how cource soever it may sound to your delicacy, that while you are without holiness, your beauty is deformit—

you are all over black and defil'd, ugly and loathsome to all holy beings, the wrath of th' great God lie's upon you, and if you die in this condition, you will be turn'd into hell, with ugly devils, to eternity." But having recorded these frightening pronouncements, little Nanny did not (like Nathaniel Mather or Betty Sewall, in an earlier generation) fall into a state of permanent terror. Instead, she goes on cheerfully to describe a little girls' party she has been to, where minuets were danced and there was a lavish supply of nuts, raisins, cakes, wine, and punch both hot and cold. "I was dressed in my yellow coat, black bib and apron, black feathers on my head, my past [paste?] comb, and all my past garnet marquesett and jet pins, together with my silver plume—my loket, rings, black collar round my neck, black mitts, and 2 or 3 yards of blue ribbin (black and blue is high tast), striped tucker and ruffels (not my best) and my silk shoes compleated my dress." And not a word about being all over black and defil'd, ugly and loathsome.

For her twelfth birthday, the little descendant of the Puritans had a "country dancing party," in which eight girls took part. She wrote about it one morning by the fire in her aunt's sitting room—and then recorded a fit of the giggles: "My aunt also says, that till I come out of an egregious fit of laughter that is apt to seize me and the violence of which I am at this present under, neither English sense, nor anything rational may be expected of me." Still, despite giggles, feathers, and dancing, she had a Puritan dedication to getting her schoolwork done. And of the Church of England clergy she remarked, "Uncle says they all have popes in their bellies." On Christmas Eve she wrote, "Tomorrow will be a holiday, so the pope and his associates have ordained. . . ." And a day or two later, "I kept Christmas at home this year, and did a very good day's work, aunt says so."

This fashionable child was fashionable in her given name, too, by the way. To have two given names, the second a surname,

32

was a custom that began about 1760, the time of Anna Green Winslow's birth. Before that, biblical names had predominated among Calvinists, together with such concoctions as Waitstill, Thankful, Increase, and Seeth ("The Lord Seeth"). In the South, old English favorites like Katharine, Jane, Henry, William, and Richard predominated. George became popular with the advent of the Hanoverian kings of England, and so did the names of members of the royal family, such as Frederick, Amelia, and Caroline.

During the eighteenth century, the general level of education declined, both north and south. But upper-class children were expected to be literate, and learning became one of the ways of distinguishing sheep from goats on a social level. A favorite sampler verse, painstakingly embroidered by eighteenth-century little girls, was this one:

> Next unto God, dear Parents, I address
> Myself to you, in humble Thankfulness.
> For all your Care and Charge on me bestowed,
> The means of learning unto me allowed.
> Go on! I pray, and let me still Pursue
> Such Golden Arts the Vulgar never knew.

The ambitious child who stitched these thoughts had probably read not only the Bible, Foxe's *Book of Martyrs*, and Wigglesworth's "Day of Doom," but had also put her nose into Milton, Pope, Addison, and the weekly newspaper.

Good penmanship—surely not a key to Heaven—was highly prized. "I would intreet you to endeavour daily to Improve yourself in writing and spelling," wrote one anxious father to his son at Princeton, in 1749. "They are very ornimentall to a scholar and the want of them is an exceeding great Blemish."

Parents were prone to push "likely" children into very early accomplishment. Eliza Pinckney, of South Carolina, wrote that she intended to buy her son a set of alphabet blocks so that he might "play himself into learning. . . . You perceive we begin betimes for he is not yet four months old." Later Mrs. Pinckney recorded proudly that "he can tell his letters in any book without hesitation, and begins to spell before he is two years old." After this child grew up and became a Revolutionary General, he complained that babyhood prodding had been a mistake and might well have had an opposite effect from the one intended.

Little Jane Turrell, born in 1708 to President Turrell of Harvard, knew her alphabet at two, her catechism at three, and was reading Cicero and Homer in the original at an age when modern children are wading through *Dick and Jane.* True, she was exceptional. For most little girls, "such Golden Arts the Vulgar never knew" were more apt to be embroidery, lacemaking, fan-painting, and the like. The quality of public education, where it existed, was so poor that if parents wanted to make scholars of their children, they had to see to it themselves. Whether they did or not, as the century wore on the children of upwardly mobile Congregationalists, Presbyterians, Dutch Reformeds, and Quakers began to join Anglican children in learning to dance and play the spinet, and in watching Punch and Judy shows and playing with store-bought toys. After 1740, or thereabouts, rather jolly children's books began to appear in England and were straightway imported in quantity by the colonies. One particular favorite, reprinted many times on both sides of the Atlantic, was *Nurse Truelove—Designed for a present to every little Boy who would become a great Man and ride upon a Fine Horse; and to every little Girl who would become a Great Woman and ride in a Governour's gilt coach.*" What worldliness! Imagine Cotton Mather's distress if he could have seen his grandchildren engrossed in *Nurse Truelove.* But, as things never change in an orderly fashion, there were still plenty of oldtime Puritans left in New England who restricted their children's light reading to *Deaths of Pious Children* and who wished Mather could come back from the grave and threaten the "rising generation."

Another great favorite was *The Little Pretty Pocket Book*. It contained moral tales for the young and advice on conduct ("All good Boys and Girls take Care to learn their Lessons and read in a pretty Manner; which makes everybody *admire* them."). For parents, there was advice on child care: "The Grand Design in the Nurture of Children is to make them Strong, Hardy, Healthy, Virtuous, Wise, and Happy; and these good Purposes are not to be obtained without some Care and Management in their Infancy." An earlier generation would have put "virtuous" first and left out "happy."

The Little Pretty Pocket Book and the rest were just big enough for a pocket. Peddlers or chapmen sold them, hence they were known as chapbooks. Some of these books were copied from adult histories, travel memoirs, and so on, and for the first time made all kinds of lore readily available for a few pence. Children on lonely farms eagerly awaited the visit of the chapman.

After a while, Americans began to try their luck as authors. *The New Gift for Children* (Boston, 1762) is believed to be the first storybook for children written in America. It is subtitled *Delightful and Entertaining Stories*, and in comparison with Janeway's tales of the deathbed, the adjectives are justified. A typical one tells of Miss Fanny Goodwill, whose "parents took great pains to improve her mind, so that before she was seven years old she could read and talk and work like a little woman" (as well as like the ideal eighteenth-century colonial child). Miss Fanny's Papa took her on his knees, "kiss'd and told her how very much he lov'd her; and then, smiling, and taking hold of her hand, My dear Fanny, said he, take care never to tell a lye, and then I shall always love you as well as I do now." He went on to say that "there is something noble and generous in owning our errors,"

35

but that "the lyar is a wretch, whom nobody trusts, nobody regards, nobody pities." "Indeed Papa," said Miss Fanny, "I would not be such a creature for all the world."

"You are very good, my little *charmer*," said her Papa and kiss'd her again." Papa's lesson is put to the test that very day, when Miss Fanny stays too late at a friend's house and is advised by a servant to "invent a story to excuse herself." Like a more famous eighteenth-century colonial child who was growing up at the same time, Miss Fanny cannot tell a lie.

Reading the Bible aloud had always been a custom in colonial families. By the mid-eighteenth century, family reading sessions included nonreligious works and even novels. One could buy specially abridged, family versions of *Pamela* and *Tom Jones*. They were abridged to omit long descriptive passages, but not censored—the lively adventures of Tom or the sexual perils of Pamela were not thought unsuitable for young ears. A hundred years or so later, students of social history were apt to register shock at certain aspects of colonial child rearing. Julian Hawthorne, for instance, wrote, "The children of the eighteenth century were urged to grow up almost before they were short-coated"; and Mrs. Rosamund Halsey, whose *Forgotten Books of the Nursery* appeared in 1911, remarked sadly, "the texture of the life of an old-fashioned child was of coarser weave than is pleasant to contemplate. How else could elders and guardians have placed without a scruple such books [as *Tom Jones*, etc.] in the hands of children?"

Little Anna Green Winslow observed the seamy side of life at firsthand. She describes in her diary the exploits of one Betty Smith, a Boston bad girl. "No sooner was the 29th Regiment encamp'd upon the common but Miss Betty took herself among them (as the Irish say) and there she stay'd with Bill Pinchion and awhile." Later, Betty was arrested for stealing and was brought in a wheeled cage to the whipping post on State Street, where thirty lashes were administered to her bare back. The place of public punishment was next door to a school. It was considered salutory for children to watch people being punished and to know what they had done to deserve it; likewise, to taunt them and throw rotten eggs at them. Public whippings and pilloryings continued in Boston until 1803.

Public executions, which took place outside of the town, were also attended by children—not for their entertainment but as an important form of moral instruction. Judge Sewall speaks in his diary of a hanging attended by many women and children, who walked from the town to the place of execution, following the condemned. A minister was in attendance and preached beneath the gallows, exhorting the young people present to take warning from the horrible example before them (the hanging of a pirate). Sewall writes that the sigh of the crowd at the moment of the prisoner's death could be heard in Boston, several miles away.

Such occasions were repeated throughout the eighteenth century; but by Nanny Winslow's time, only children of "the poorer sort" attended. There were street gangs in Boston—rival factions of ragged, dirty, and lousy children, who sometimes fought pitched battles with flying stones and bricks. A little Brahmin child like Nanny would not have been allowed to associate with them.

In a negative way, Calvinist doctrine taught equality: all mankind was vile. But while shared vileness might unite magistrates and beggars in the next world, it was not to be used as an excuse for "leveling" in this one. One might feel deep concern for the souls of street urchins to the extent of contributing to "ragged schools" where they might learn to read the Bible, yet ignore their temporal state. Charity was not an important virtue in those days. Nearly everyone on both sides of the Atlantic shared the view that the poor and hungry were that way

37

because they had "bad blood" (we might say "inferior genes"), or were paying for the sins of their fathers. In either case, their situation was God's will.

From the beginning, New England towns protected themselves from having to cope with more than their share of indigents by the Warning Out System. Strangers in a town were closely scrutinized, and if suspected of being without means of support, were ordered to leave at once or be whipped out at the tail of a cart. Indigent residents of a town, if able-bodied, were ordered to work for their neighbors. Their children were placed in families as bond-servants. Any family could use an extra hand, and since all children worked there was not much practical difference between children who lived with their parents and children who were bound out as servants. In New England the law still required that heads of households must, with equal care, educate their own children, their servants, and their apprentices. And the tithing-man made sure that no heads of households mistreated, neglected, or overindulged their dependents, at least not flagrantly. Chastisement was expected—the Bible urged it and every father kept a supple birch switch for the purpose. However, colonial court records show instances of child servants who were incapacitated by cruel punishment, or deprived of food, bedding, and clothing, and in such cases the court fined the offender and placed the child elsewhere. In one case, parents were fined for leaving their small children alone in the house.

In 1685, Samuel Sewall noted in his diary that a neighbor had found an infant abandoned on his doorstep. "So far as I can hear," Sewall wrote, "this is the first Child that ever was in such a manner exposed in Boston." "Dropping" children (as it was called), while very common in England, remained rare in America until after the Revolution. Children, even bastards, were too useful to throw away.

From time to time some untoward calamity produced a

flood of orphans. The various colonial wars left many orphans to place, and periodic epidemics of smallpox played havoc with families. Sometimes childless people adopted the orphan child of relatives or neighbors; but it was unheard-of to adopt a child of strangers or of unknown parentage, because one did not know what his "blood" was. Child-adoption did not become common until this century.

But orphans, foundlings, and bound children might, with hard work and luck, grow up to become leading citizens. A case in point is that of Agnes Surriage, a beautiful Marblehead girl who, while scrubbing her master's front steps, attracted the eye of a rich Englishman, Sir Henry Frankland. At sixteen she became his mistress—and here the story deviates from the approved Puritan standard: she neither repented nor was struck dead. She lived with Sir Harry for a number of years, traveling in Europe. They chanced to be in Lisbon in 1755, during the great earthquake, which gave Agnes the opportunity of saving her lover's life. He showed his gratitude by marrying her and they returned to New England, where they lived in great style and, apparently, under no particular moral cloud. Things had certainly changed since the early days of New England, when adultery was punishable by death.

Old Increase Mather, surviving from those righteous times into the slack 1720s, called for a revival of piety in the rising generation. He pondered the problem of why godly parents should have ungodly children, and concluded that it was because all are born sinful and because Satan is always at work and because "eminent servants of God" are, unfortunately, mortal and must die—even as Moses, Paul, and Increase Mather. "A godly man can no more make his children godly than he can Raise the Dead out of their Graves," he concluded. Thinking back to the days of his boyhood, seventy years before, he remembered having heard a preacher say that he had not heard a profane oath nor seen a drunkard in New England for seven years. "I must Weep," said old Dr. Mather, "and I now do it with a Loud Voice, for what I see."

And what did he see? He saw young people of good old Puritan families wearing frivolous clothing and "horrid wigs"; he saw them going to ale houses and feasting on Christmas Day; he saw children of his congregation playing with Church of England children; and he saw young people following their fancy regarding matrimony instead of adhering to the old Puritan principle of first deciding to marry and then looking for a sober, godly prospect whom, with an effort of will, one might succeed in loving, and of whom one's parents fully approved. So far had things changed in three or four generations that a descendant of John Winthrop went on record with the statement, "It has been the way and custom of the country for young folks to choose, and where there is noe visible exception everybody approves it."

When Increase Mather had been a boy, Massachusetts law had forbidden young men "to insinuate into the affections of young maidens, by coming to them in places and seasons unknown to their parents for such end . . . ," and another law, in Connecticut, had ordered them not to "inveigle or draw the affection of any maid, whether it be by speech, writing, message, company-keeping, unnecessary familiarity, disorderly night-meetings, sinful dalliance, or gifts." In Connecticut, in 1660, a pair of teenagers had been brought into court, charged with having sat with their arms around each other—"and hee kissed her and shee kissed him, or they kissed one another, continuing in this posture about half an hour." Ninety years later, in 1750, Connecticut was still having trouble with the young: a Justice of the Peace recorded fines for "smiling and larfing" in meeting. The offender had also been "puling the heir of his naybor— playing with her Hand and fingers at her heir."

Betrothal was a legal contract, involving dowries and

settlements, with a good deal of haggling between in-laws. For the purest Puritans, a marriage was a civil affair, performed very simply at home by a magistrate. Dutch brides were married at home, but not simply—the occasion being marked by a three-day feast and happy uproar. The bride wore white—a custom that eventually was to become nationwide. In the Old World, young married couples traditionally moved in with in-laws. Here, with a continent at their disposal, a young couple might leave for the frontier; or perhaps the bridegroom would spend his betrothal days building a new house on his father's land.

For an engaged couple to cohabit before marriage was sinful, but only half as sinful as to cohabit when *not* engaged (in New England, the legal fine was only half as much). In 1721, the Reverend Joseph Sewall, a son of the old Judge, addressed a sermon to the young as follows: "Yes, for Persons that contract an intimate acquaintance with the purpose of Marriage to come together before it be consummated is not to be accounted a small sin: No! It is a dishonor to God and a scandal to Religion." Clearly, some in his congregation must have been jumping the gun and accounting it a small sin, or Sewall would not have brought the subject up. The eighteenth-century records of New England towns show a remarkable number of seven-month firstborns. If the parents were properly married, they could rehabilitate themselves in the eyes of church and community by making public confessions in meeting. They had to stand together in the aisle, the young wife with her eyes lowered, saying nothing, and the husband doing the talking. Unmarried mothers had to speak for themselves.

Young people sometimes fell into such predicaments because of the custom of bundling. In a cold climate, where fuel was short and houses small, it was an ingenious method of courtship. (We do not hear of it in New England until the eighteenth century, when the idea may have been brought over by Welsh immigrants. The Dutch along the Hudson had a similar custom, called queesting.) Fully clothed, a young unmarried couple spent a cozy but chaste evening in bed together. For added security, a board was usually introduced between them, and the girl's mother was likely to tie or even sew her daughter into her clothing. But in spite of these precautions, bundling sometimes led to unplanned consequences. In 1781, a Groton minister, noting the number of confessions of fornication he had been hearing lately, urged the young people of Groton to give up bundling.

A British officer, Thomas Anburey, encountered the custom in a rural Massachusetts household shortly before the Revolution. He wrote, "I was convinced in how innocent a view the Americans look upon that indelicate custom they call bundling." In the house where Anburey was billeted, there were two beds and the young officer was invited to bundle in one of them with his host's daughter, Jemima.

> I was much astonished at such a proposal, and offered to sit up **all** night, when Jonathan immediately replied, "Oh, la! Mr. Ensign, you won't be the first man our Jemima has bundled with, will it, Jemima?", when little Jemima, who, by the bye, was a very pretty black-eyed girl of about sixteen or seventeen, archly replied, "No, Father, by many, but it will be with the first Britisher." In this dilemma, what could I do?—the smiling invitation of pretty Jemima—the eye—the lip, the—Lord ha' mercy, where am I going to?—but wherever I may be going to now, I did not go to bundle with her—in the same room with her father and mother, my kind *host* and *hostess* too!—I thought of that—thought of more besides—to struggle with the passions of nature; to clasp Jemima in my arms—to—do what? you'll ask—why, to do—nothing! for if amid all these temptations the lovely Jemima had melted into kindness, she had been an outcast from the world—treated with contempt, abused by violence, and left perhaps to perish! . . . Suppose how great the test of virtue must be or how cold the American constitution when this unaccountable custom is in hospitable repute, and perpetual practice.

After houses grew larger and the average rural family more prosperous and more sophisticated, bundling became improper —indeed, so much so that it is rare to find a written record of it. If it were not for Ensign Anburey's reminiscences, a few denunciatory sermons, and two broadsides of 1787, we might wonder whether bundling ever really happened.

The broadsides, published in Boston, are "bundling songs" —one pro and one con. The anonymous poet who favored bundling turned to the Bible for guidance and could find nothing there against it ("The sacred book says wives they took, it don't say how they courted, / Whether that they in bed did lay, or by the fire sported."). The other point of view attacks bundling as certain to lead to trouble (". . . bundler's clothes are no defense / unruly horses push the fence.").

Bundling or no bundling, visitors from Europe never ceased to be amazed at the freedom of adolescents in America. Ensign Anburey reported that a large group of young people in a Massachusetts village drove twenty miles after dark in sleighs, danced all night, and returned to their homes at dawn. "In England this would be esteemed extremely imprudent, and attended with dangerous consequences, but after what I have related respecting *bundling,* I need not say, in how innocent a view this is looked upon." Another British officer describes a "turtle frolick." He called for a young lady in Boston and drove her in a chaise to a party in Cambridge, six miles away. There, with about twenty other young people, they danced minuets and country dances, feasted on turtle, and returned home after dusk. The Frenchman Brissot de Warville, traveling through America in 1788, was astonished by the same sort of thing. "You see girls go off for a drive in the country with their sweethearts in a chaise, and their innocent pleasures are never beclouded with insulting suspicions." Another French observer, Perrin du Lac, wrote that not only did American boys and girls go to school together, but "when their public education is finished at the age of twelve or

Four New York siblings: the children of Garrett and Helena Rapalje
The New-York Historical Society

thirteen, the girls lose none of the freedom enjoyed in childhood. Their school friends, or those made elsewhere, visit them freely whether or not their parents are present." And de Chastellux noted, "It is no crime for a girl to kiss a young man; it would indeed be one for a married woman even to show a desire of pleasing."

In New York, in 1767, a nineteen-year-old theological student named Ahimaaz Harker reproved his peers in a book called *A Companion for the Young People of North America—Particularly recommended to those within the three Provinces of New-York, New-Jersey, and Pennsylvania*. He shook his head over the freedoms allowed in the practice known as "keeping company," and vehemently denounced dancing. "It is amazing," he wrote, "to see how young People will spend whole Nights in this slavish Exercise— we must be convinced of the Folly that urges us to spend whole Nights in puffing and blowing at a Dance." (But even Harker approved of dancing school, which, he believed, cultivated grace and manners.)

According to the memoirs of a Scottish woman, Mrs. Grant, who, as a child in the mid-eighteenth century, lived for several years in the Schuyler family, near Albany, Dutch children from the age of five or six went about in "companies," which were organizations, or clubs, composed of both boys and girls. Brothers and sisters did not join the same company. The children wandered the woods and fields together—"permitted to range about at full liberty in their earliest years." There were often teen-age marriages within a company. Parents were indulgent, and early marriages without permission were not infrequent. But the usual custom was for boys to remain unmarried until they were at least twenty, when they made a trading trip into the wild interior of the colony of New York in order to make enough money to set up housekeeping. Girls' dowries usually consisted of a slave or two, a bed, and some linen. As Mrs. Grant remembered it, this was a rollicking, uninhibited childhood, full

45

of family love and "company" comradeship. Boys played with girls and the highborn with the humble. The Dutch did not like the much stricter class system of their English rulers.

In the South, the "middling sort" and the poor allowed their children a good deal of freedom, and marriage was even earlier than in the North. (The first marriage recorded in any English colony took place in 1608 between a fourteen-year-old servant-girl and a boy servant not much older.) Wealthy plantation owners usually endeavored to give their children a good education and good manners, and to instill them with self-control. For a firsthand look at the life of children on a Virginia plantation, we have the diary of Philip Fithian, a young theological student from New Jersey, who, in 1774, was tutor to seven of the seventeen children of Robert Carter.

Young Mr. Fithian, a born writer, tells us all the details we want to know about, so that the large family of Carter children rise from the pages of his diary like charming and rambunctious ghosts. Fithian taught his charges in the plantation schoolhouse. While the oldest boy, aged seventeen, read Latin and began Greek, the oldest daughter, a year younger, was just beginning multiplication and division and was reading *The Spectator*. The second son, who excelled at such important Virginian accomplishments as hunting and shooting, riding, dancing, cards and "small-sword," struggled with English grammar and subtraction; while the younger children were busy with reading and spelling. All labored over their penmanship.

Outside school hours, the young people amused themselves with visits to other plantations, balls, dancing lessons, fish-feasts, barbecues, horseraces, boating, and studying various musical instruments, including the guitar and "forte-piana." They squabbled: "Fanny pull'd off her Shoe & threw at Nancy, which missed her and broke a pane of glass of our School Room." When they were naughty, Mr. Fithian corrected them by striking their hands with "smart twigs." Colonel and Mrs. Carter seem to have been in perfect command. (". . . all the Children are in remarkable subjection to their Parents.") By Fithian's Presbyterian standards, there was too much attention paid to dogs, horses, and dance steps and not enough to religion, but he commented resignedly, "How different the Manners of the People [of the South]!"

Robert Carter was the wealthiest man in Virginia, owning more than 60,000 acres and 600 slaves. Yet his plantation house, Nomini Hall, was surprisingly simple. It had four rooms on each of its two floors: downstairs, a dining-sitting room for adults and another for children, Mr. Carter's study, and a thirty-foot ballroom; upstairs, a bedroom for Mr. and Mrs. Carter, two for guests (and there were always guests), and the last for *all* the daughters, the white housekeeper, and a black maid-servant. The boys slept in an outbuilding.

Although southern Anglican children learned their catechism, said prayers, and went to church more or less regularly, they knew nothing like the religious emphasis still prevalent in the northern colonies. (Southern frontier children were likely to be Presbyterian, but there was seldom a minister or church within many miles to remind them of hellfire and damnation.) In the North, those clergymen who were most successful in reaching the young concentrated on building up their anxiety: would they go to heaven or hell?

Particularly remembered for his success in terrifying children is that towering Congregationalist, Jonathan Edwards. Edwards was born in 1703 on a frontier farm in Connecticut. His father, an itinerant preacher, and his exemplary Puritan mother were eminently concerned with the education of their numerous children, and taught Latin and Hebrew to both boys and girls. The *paterfamilias* was often away from home, but he oversaw every phase of his children's development, as is evident from this letter to his wife:

I hope thou wilt take special care of Jonathan yt he don't Learn to be rude & naughty etc. of which thee and I have lately discoursed. I wouldn't have thee venture him to ride out into ye woods with Tim. I hope God will help thee to be very carefull yt no harm happen to ye little Children by Scalding wort, whey, water, or by standing too nigh to Tim when he is cutting wood. . . . And let Esther & Betty Take their powders as Soon as the Dog Days are Over, and if they don't help Esther, talk further with ye Doctr about her for I wouldn't have her be neglected. Something else Should be done for Anne who as thou knowest is weakly. Take Care of thy Self and Dont Suckle little Jerusha too long.

When Jonathan Edwards was nine years old, he had The Experience. His father conducted yearly revivals, and, following his example, young Jonathan built what he called a "booth" on the edge of a swamp near the Edwards farm and persuaded children to assemble there to pray. He went to Yale at thirteen and at eighteen was ready for a pulpit. He never sowed even one wild oat, and unlike poor Nathaniel Mather, never lost his confidence that he was one of God's Elect. Established at Northampton, Massachusetts, he began to preach eloquently on the subject of hellfire and damnation in language reminiscent of the fiery tirades of the Puritan heyday. Many of his sermons were directed to children. "God is angry with you every day," he told them. ". . . How dreadful to have God angry with you. How dreadful ill it be to be in Hell among the devils and know that you must be there to all Eternity. . . . Then . . . you won't play together any more but will be damned together, will cry out with weeping and wailing and gnashing of teeth together."

These strong words produced many conversions. Edwards's favorite convert was little Phebe Bartlett, who, at the age of four began to retire several times a day for secret prayer. One day her mother heard her praying in a loud, distressed voice, "Pray Blessed Lord, give me Salvation! I pray beg pardon all my sins!"

Her mother asked her if she feared damnation, and she said, "Yes, I am afraid I shall go to Hell." In "anguish of spirit" she rocked her body to and fro and refused to be comforted. Then, quite suddenly, she stopped, smiled, and announced, "Mother, the Kingdom of Heaven is come to me! . . . I can find God now! I love God!"

Her mother asked, "Better than Father and Mother?"

"Yes."

"Better than little sister Rachel?"

"Yes—better than anything."

She then expressed a fear that her sisters would go to hell, and counseled them to "prepare to die." She said she could hardly wait for the Sabbath to come.

"Why, to see the fine folks?"

"No, to hear Mr. Edwards preach."

Edwards relates all this in his book *A Faithful Narrative of the Surprising Work of God,* and adds an account of the good he accomplished among the adolescents of Northampton. "Licentiousness for some Years greatly prevailed among the Youth . . . [who were] addicted to Nightwalking, and frequenting the Tavern and lewd practices." Boys and girls had been accustomed to get together "for Mirth and Jollity which they called Frolicks; and they would often spend the greater part of the Night in them." By reminding them that God abhorred them and was holding them over the pit of hell "much as one holds a spider or some loathsome insect over the fire," Edwards soon put a stop to all that. He held sway in Northampton for two or three years, until his congregation grew restive and finally rebelled when he ordered them not to read a wicked novel called *The Midwife Rightly Instructed.* He was then ousted from his pulpit.

In one respect, at least, the children of the eighteenth century were very much like those of the preceding generations. When it came to showing respect for their parents, they toed the line—as we have seen in the case of the Carter children. "Honor thy Father and Mother" was, after all, a Commandment, and all the Commandments were taken seriously. In New England, disobedient children could still be punished by a public whipping. Not that there were no black sheep—even Cotton Mather had a black-sheep son, Increase (known as Cresy), who drank and caroused and was accused of fathering an illegitimate child and finally got his comeuppance by drowning at sea. But even Cresy showed his father every outward respect and gave him nothing but humble thanks for all his lecturing and nagging.

The Little Pretty Pocket Book set forth some rules of behavior for children toward their parents, reprinted without change from an Elizabethan etiquette manual. "Make a Bow always when you come Home, and be instantly uncovered. Never sit in the Presence of thy Parents or Strangers without bidding; though no strangers be present. If thou passest by thy Parents at any Place where thou seest them, either by themselves or with Company, bow towards them. Bear with Meekness and Patience and without Murmuring or Sullenness thy Parents' Reproofs or Corrections. Nay, though it should happen that they be causeless or undeserved."

Parents seem to have felt a constant compulsion to correct their children. Here is a Boston minister, Benjamin Colman, writing, in 1718, to his nine-year-old daughter:

> I charge you to pray daily and read your Bible and fear to sin. Be very dutiful to your Mother, and respectful to every Body. . . . Be very humble and modest, womanly and discreet. Take care of your health and as you love me do not eat green apples. Drink sparingly of water, except the day be warm. When I last saw you, you were too shamefaced; look people in the face, speak freely and behave decently. . . .

The admonition to look people in the face and speak freely marked a significant change, typical of America; English etiquette advice for children had always instructed them to keep their eyes lowered when speaking to older people and to speak only if spoken to.

But the important message that adults wished to convey to children was that they must be good and mind their parents. Abigail Adams wrote to her son John Quincy, an exemplary boy who scarcely ever gave his parents a moment's anxiety, "I would rather you should have found your grave in the ocean you have crossed, or that an untimely death crop you in your infant years, than see you an immoral, profligate, or graceless child." In another letter she counseled him always to rate his parents' judgment above his own.

The colonies contributed little original thinking to the literature of child care, but they paid a great deal of attention to what came to them from abroad. Perhaps the most widely read of all works on child care before the nineteenth century was John Locke's *Some Thoughts Concerning Education*, which first appeared in 1689, and was plagiarized extensively throughout the eighteenth century. It seems surprising that so eminent and lofty a thinker as John Locke—and a bachelor, at that—should have concerned himself with the feeding, bathing, and toilet training of young children. But so he did, and his book became the equivalent of Dr. Spock's *Baby and Child Care* wherever there were conscientious parents who knew how to read.

Despite the fact that he rarely entered a nursery, the distinguished bachelor was a mine of advice on the feeding of children—and most of it was good. The very young, he said, should eat plain food only: milk, milk-pottage, gruel, flummery (a plain pudding), and not much sugar, spice, or salt. "The best breakfast for my young master" is plain brown bread; between meals, if he must have something, dry bread only. He pointed out that the Romans had only one regular meal a day through Caesar's time, after which they became corrupted by eastern luxuries. "A gentleman in any age ought to be so bred as to be fitted to bear arms and be a soldier. But he that in this breeds his son so as if he designed him to sleep over his life in the plenty and ease of a full fortune he intends to leave him, little considers the examples he has seen, or the age he lives in." (This advice was particularly well received in America, where fortunes fluctuated wildly.)

A Locke child, like a Spock child, was to be kept away from candy and given dried fruit and ripe apples and pears instead. Ripe strawberries, cherries, gooseberries, and currants met with Locke's approval, but he thought melons, peaches, plums, and grapes had "a very tempting taste in a very unwholesome juice." As for drink, it should be small beer only, and that only with a meal or piece of bread. "Not being permitted to drink without eating, will prevent the custom of having the cup often at his nose; a dangerous beginning, and preparation to good-fellow-ship. Men often bring habitual hunger and thirst on themselves by custom. Because nurses are apt to soothe children with drinking in the night, the habit is hard to break." Contrary to the prevalent English (and colonial) custom, children should not be given wine or strong drink.

Early to bed and early to rise was Locke's maxim. A child should get plenty of sleep and become accustomed to a hard bed rather than feathers. ". . . he is very unfortunate who can take his cordial only in his mother's fine gilt cup, and not in a wooden dish."

Locke wrote that for personal reasons, he had looked into the matter of how to make habitual "the peristaltic motion of the guts . . . and not finding the cure of it in books, I set my thoughts on work. . . . Then I guessed that if a man, after his first eating in the morning, would presently solicit nature and try whether he could strain himself so as to obtain a stool, he might in time, by constant application, bring it to be habitual." Experiment proved him right. And he therefore recommended that every small child, daily after breakfast, "be set upon the stool, as if disburdening were as much in his power as filling his belly; and let not him or his maid know anything to the contrary . . . and if he be forced to endeavor, by being hindered from his play or eating again till he has been effectually at stool, or at least done his utmost, I doubt not but in a little while it will become natural to him." No doubt many children had been put through this process for centuries before John Locke, but he was the first to write about it.

Some of Locke's theories seem somewhat bizarre today, but they, too, were widely followed. He wanted children bathed in cold water only, winter and summer, and "I will also advise his feet to be washed every day in cold water, and to have his shoes so thin that they might leak and let in water, whenever he comes near it." These drastic measures would, he believed, prevent "the mischiefs that usually attend accidental taking wet in the feet in those who are bred otherwise." He pointed to the barefoot poor, who, he said, "take no more cold or harm by [wet feet] than if they were wet in their hands"; and he quoted an ancient anecdote about a Scythian, who, when asked by an Athenian how he could go about naked in frost and snow, returned, "How can you endure your face exposed to the sharp winter air?" "My face is used to it," said the Athenian. "Think me all face," replied the Scythian.

Locke was undoubtedly trying to combat the age-old custom of keeping children airless and nearly smothered. Unfortunately, he went to the other extreme and many of his readers followed his advice to the letter. For example, Josiah Quincy, born in Boston in 1772, was taken into the cellar every morning of his childhood and plunged into a tub of freshly pumped spring water. (True, he lived to a ripe old age.) And although Locke never went so far as to say that cold baths would cure illness, sick children were often "dipped." A letter written in New England in 1769 described the following cure for rickets:

53

> If you dip your Child, Do it in this manner: viz: naked in ye morning head foremost in Cold Water, don't dress it Immediately, but let it be made warm in ye Cradle and sweat at least half an Hour moderately. Do this three mornings going and if one or both feet are Cold while other parts sweat (which is sometimes ye Case) Let a little blood be taken out of ye feet ye second Morning and yt wil cause them to sweat afterwards. Before ye dip ye Child, give it some Snakewood and Saffern Steep'd in Rum and Water . . .

Aside from these drastic, newfangled treatments, a lot of medieval remedies and superstitious rites were still in use in the colonies. For example, a newborn had a scarlet cloth laid on his head to protect him from harm. When first moved, he was carried upstairs with silver and gold in his hands—so that he would rise in the world. Although John Locke advised that any baby with hair should go capless, most infants wore a thickly padded cap, called a biggin, day and night, winter and summer. A baby who fussed much got Daffy's Elixir, a commercial pacifier. Like other "soothing drops," it contained opium, and a slight overdose would render him pacified for good.

Gin and rum were another form of soothing drops for infants. Abigail Adams writes of how she rescued the orphan child of acquaintances from its wet nurse, who "made the poor thing sick by taking it out in the evening and giving it Rum, the Nurse says to make it sleep." Mrs. Adams indignantly took the baby home with her and eventually arranged for it to be adopted by relatives of its deceased father.

This child was lucky. To be sent to live with a wet nurse was likely to be a death sentence. Child-care books warned against it and also counseled against leaving children in the care of household servants. Both practices were usual in England but unusual in the colonies. After the Revolution, they became even more unusual, partly because wet nurses and servants were notoriously unsatisfactory and also because the new United States looked askance on all things British. The new Americans were exceedingly patriotic. They wanted to prove to the world that the United States was a superior place and they took very seriously the task of filling it with a superior rising generation.

The Swedish traveler Peter Kalm, writing of Pennsylvania in 1750, observed, "It is nothing uncommon to see little children giving sprightly and ready answers to questions that are proposed to them, so that they seem to have as much understanding as old men." Foreigners were apt to call this sort of thing sheer impudence, but to most Americans it was a sign of initiative and independence—qualities admired as much in a child as in a nation. And far from allowing children to run wild, most parents knew that child rearing was a serious matter, even though they were not sure how to go about it.

It has been said that when Americans perceive a need for something—whether it is a plow, a doctrine, or a rocket to the moon—they do not rest until they have produced it. Let us see, then, what systems they produced for rearing children.

PART TWO

The Nineteenth Century

Jumping rope
Girl's Own Book by Mrs. Child
(Boston: American Stationer's Company, 1837)

3
THE FEDERAL CHILD

Bedelia Smithers is my name
America my nation
Wilmington is my earthly home
And Heaven my destination
(*sampler verse, 1810*)

WHAT A SPLENDID LITTLE FELLOW IS FIVE-YEAR-OLD BILLY! Not only does he know his catechism but he can also recite the Preamble to the Constitution. His parents are intent on making him a model American citizen; and although they have read enough child-care advice to know that they ought not to let Billy show off, they cannot resist having him recite to some of their friends an "address" he has learned by heart from the new *Children's Magazine.* "Americans!" declaims Billy, standing on the best parlor chair. "Place constantly before your eyes the deplorable scenes of your servitude and the enchanting picture of your deliverance. Begin with the infant in his cradle; let the first word he lisps be *Washington.*"

It is nearly as essential for Billy to be patriotic as to be religious. Children's books imported from England no longer seem quite suitable for little Americans. A child's history of the world that contains a woodcut portrayal of George III has the "III" deleted and "Washington" substituted under the picture. (No matter about the likeness—it does not greatly resemble either George, anyway.) *Cries of New York*, printed in that city, has stolen its engravings from *Cries of London*, but gives different names to some of the wares being cried through the streets— corn, watermelon, and clams, for instance, instead of cockles, mussels, and hot cross buns. Educators are hard at work producing an American speller, an American dictionary, American histories, and, of course, American advice on child rearing.

By the end of the century there are only two widely circulated books on the latter subject. Of these, the better known is Dr. John Witherspoon's *Letters on Education*. Dr. Witherspoon, president of Princeton College, was born in Scotland, but is impeccably American by virtue of having signed the Declaration of Independence. Most of his advice is of the traditional authoritarian variety. "There is not a more disgusting sight than the impotent rage of a parent who has no authority," he warns at the outset, adding that in the army and navy, "those who keep the strictest discipline give the fewest strokes." To establish parental authority early, he recommends, "Once a day, take something from them." Parents who begin doing this when each child is eight or nine months old may well have accomplished the training process by twelve or fourteen months and will never have to resort to the rod. (For Witherspoon, as for virtually all eighteenth-century people, a child is as trainable at one year as he will ever be. The concept of stages of development was still far in the future.)

Dr. Witherspoon continues:

It is surprising to think how early children will discover the weak side of their parents, and what ingenuity they will shew in obtaining their favour or avoiding their displeasure. . . . There are some families . . . in which the parents are literally and properly obedient to their children, are forced to do things against their will and chidden if they discover the least backwardness to comply. If you know none such, I am sure I do.

He cautioned against loss of parental dignity through rage or resentment:

Everyone would be sensible that for a magistrate to discover an intemperate rage in pronouncing sentence against a criminal, would be highly indecent.

To succeed, parents must be sincerely religious and sincerely in agreement as to the goals they wish to reach and the means for reaching them. Servants, if any, must be strictly instructed and overseen. The good doctor has no objection to small rewards, such as toys or candy or words of praise, but warns parents to avoid the predicament of the Roman emperors with their bread and circuses. And remember, he adds kindly, parents are sure to do wrong occasionally.

Even though little of Witherspoon's advice departs from the prerevolutionary standard, he does say that in his opinion the discipline of an earlier age was too severe—"in many instances terrible and disgusting." And he puts his finger on the most awkward drawback to any system of child raising: There is "great diversity in the temper and disposition of children" and "no less in the penetration, prudence and resolution of parents." Most writers of child-care advice, even today, seem to feel that bringing up a child is like following a recipe: do exactly what the book tells you and the cake will never fall.

The Memoirs of the Bloomsgrove Family, by Enos Hitchcock (1790), is subtitled, "Sentiments on a Mode of Domestic Education Suited to the Present State of Society, Government and Manners in the United States of America, and dedicated to

Mrs. Washington." Although Hitchcock was a clergyman (it would be another generation at least before lay people would presume to give advice in this field), he was out to make good citizens for the United States as well as for heaven.

To make his advice more readable, Dr. Hitchcock invented a model family—Mr. and Mrs. Bloomsgrove and their two children, Rozella and Osander. (Fancy or classical-sounding names were very much in fashion.) The Bloomsgroves lived on a pleasant farm and were apparently very prosperous; but though they might well have afforded nurses and tutors, they took personal charge of their children. "In America, children are generally reared up in a domestic state, and by their parents; few are put to nurse; fewer still committed to the care of private tutors, or subtle and vicious servants." This was the regrettable custom in England, where the upper classes were apt to be indolent. ". . . It is to be regretted," Dr. Hitchcock wrote, "that anything similar to this should ever have crept into America; where an estate, however large, seldom passes beyond a third generation; because that generation is brought up in indolence, and indulged in extravagant expenses." Some parents, he went on, believed that work would make boys servile and girls "indelicate." But the old adage applies: He that will not work shall not eat. And he cites the case of a once proud and flourishing family "sunk under the weight of infirmity, con-tracted by indolence, and mingled with the common mass of inert matter."

To preserve Rozella and Osander from such a fate, they were brought up very plainly. The parent Bloomsgroves had evidently read John Locke's *Some Thoughts Concerning Education,* for they believed in cold baths, dry bread, and wet feet. "Rozella is suffered to wet her feet while at play, and slide on the ice." They had no bought toys, but made their own—tops and bows and arrows for Osander, dolls and their clothing for Rozella. Each had a little garden. "Rozella cannot dig her garden, this would be too masculine an employment for a little girl—but she can pull out the weeds." Their clothing was light and they went bareheaded, just as Locke would have advised. A head exposed to the air "gathers strength . . . the business of thinking, reflecting and reasoning will be carried on with greater activity and vigor."

In one respect, Dr. Hitchcock differed from the norm—he did not believe in set mealtimes or forced eating. "The habit of eating at a particular hour, when we rise into a family state, becomes convenient; business, company, and the order of society, render it unavoidable; but it cannot be necessary that children should be compelled to eat then, or to suspend eating at other times." If Osander complained of hunger, he was "tried with a piece of dry bread or fair water." If these were accepted, his parents assumed he was hungry and gave him a meal.

Little Americans, Hitchcock went on, must learn to regulate the passions—else they will not "patiently submit to the restraint of government. . . . From such undisciplined members arise domestic animosities, discord between neighbors, opposition to lawful authority and disturbances in society." Mr. and Mrs. Bloomsgrove restrain their own passions in order to be good examples. Mrs. Bloomsgrove ushers insects out the door instead of swatting them, and she takes care not to let the children see that she is terrified of thunderstorms. No ghost or goblin tales are allowed in the house, nor any illiterate servant talk. Though there are servants in the house, the children are rarely left alone with them. Mr. and Mrs. Bloomsgrove act in perfect accord, knowing intuitively how to raise their little American citizens. This is fortunate, for the child-care books for sale in the shops are all "suited to a distant meridian."

There was an element of buoyancy and optimism in early Federal life and it reflected itself in the young people. We have the letters of Eliza Southgate, a teen-age miss who wrote to her parents from boarding school about 1800. Eliza is bright and gay, as well as sentimental and patriotic—a model daughter of Columbia. At the time of her letters, she is in mourning for George Washington, wearing on her arm a black ribbon with a line of memorial verse painted on it. Some of her friends are in full mourning. But her letters are far from melancholy.

> You have always treated me more like a companion than a daughter and therefore would make allowance for the volatile expressions I often make use of. I never felt the least restraint in company with my Parents which would induce me to stifle my gaiety, and you have kindly permitted me to rant over all my nonsense uncorrected, and I positively believe it has never injured.

Of an older woman, she remarks, "Her manners are such as would have been admired fifty years ago. There is too much appearance of whalebone and buckram to please the depraved taste of the present age." Girls of Eliza's generation no longer wore stays, but, instead, the light, filmy attire copied from postrevolutionary France.

Eliza accepts what freedom she has and resigns herself to what she cannot have. She regrets that women have the liberty of refusing to marry men they don't like, but not of selecting those they do. "I have firmness enough to brave the sneers of the world and live an old maid if I never find one I can love." Brave, yes, but she is no rebel: "Reputation undoubtedly is of great importance to all, but to a female 'tis everything—once lost, 'tis *forever* lost."

It was not long before Eliza found the right man, married, and became a typical Federal mother. From New York City, she wrote her parents in Maine of sending her little son out walking "frequently when 'tis so cold it quite makes the tears come; he trudges along with leading very well in the street, he never takes cold. He goes to bed at six o'clock away in the room in the third story . . . without fire or candle, and there he sleeps till Phoebe goes to bed with him. You know I am a great enemy to letting children sleep with a fire in the room; 'tis the universal practice here." (Dr. Hitchcock would have approved of the cold room, but disapproved of Phoebe.) But charming Eliza did not live to see whether her child-care theories were successful. Like so many American girls of her period, she contracted tuberculosis and died young.

Another young mother of the early Federal period was the beautiful Nancy Shippen, who, as a girl of sixteen, had been courted by a French diplomat but chose instead a member of the vastly wealthy Livingston family of New York. It was a miserable choice. Her husband turned out to be a profligate and Nancy left him. As women had no rights then, her daughter was taken away from her. In return for not pressing for a divorce, she was allowed to see the child occasionally. For these longed-for periods, Nancy wrote down her own rules for child care, which show the trend of the time away from rigid authoritarianism and toward a more gentle regime:

> First, study well her constitution and genius. If she be a brisk witty child, do not applaud her too much. If she be a dull heavy child, do not discourage her at all. Never let her converse with servants. . . . Acquaint her in the most pleasant insinuating manner with the sacred History, nor let it seem her lesson, but her recreation. . . . Use her to rise betimes in the morning and set before her in the most winning manner an order for the whole day.

Change and experimentation were in the air, and while children were still brought up with a strong emphasis on religion, the young generation who lived in or near the towns and cities and were exposed to the exciting new atmosphere were often noticeably restive. For example, there was Henry James, senior, father of William James and Henry James, who was born in 1811 and was brought up in Albany in a strict Presbyterian family. He

hated what he called the "not-to-do" prohibitions of Sunday—
"not to play, not to dance nor to sing, not to read storybooks, nor
to con over our school lessons for Monday even; not to whistle,
not to ride the pony, nor to take a walk in the country nor a swim
in the river; nor, in short to do anything which nature specially
craved." When he grew up, he, like many another product of the
Federal age, did not inflict a wrathful God or a Sabbath-strict
religion upon his own children.

But for country youngsters, life went on very much as it had
before the Revolution—and, according to the census of 1790,
more than 97 percent of Americans lived in the country. Enoch
Pond, born in 1791, who grew up to become a leading theologian
and defender of oldtime Calvinism, wrote memoirs that show
only affectionate memories of a childhood brimming with
religion. Near the village of Wrentham, Massachusetts, three
generations of the Pond family lived together in their farmhouse,
almost independent of the world. The children worked constantly—never to exhaustion, but never idle. "The flood of
juvenile books had not then burst upon the country," wrote old
Dr. Pond. "We fed our minds on the same intellectual food as did
our parents and it stimulated our thoughts and enlarged our
mental powers." A religious revival in 1804 deepened his interest
in religion, but with true Puritan zeal he looked back on himself
as a sinful youth. ". . . I became more wicked than I had ever
been before. I attended church as usual; but was fond of gay
company, was restive under family restraint and even learned,
when among my companions, to use profane language." Enoch
Pond was a colonial child in a Federal age, but there were many
like him, and they grew up to extend the old ways even a
generation further. Pond's son remembered his father talking
him out of wanting to attend dancing school. "To this day I feel
the influence of his description and disgust at dancing," the
younger Pond wrote in the 1870s.

Families like the Ponds needed no child-care manual—they had one in the Bible:

> Withhold not correction from the child: for if thou beatest him with the rod, he shall not die.

> . . . a child left to himself bringeth his mother to shame.

> The eye that mocketh at his father and despiseth to obey his mother, the ravens of the valley shall pick it out, and the young eagles shall eat it.

And, of course, best known and simplest, the no-nonsense message paraphrased from Solomon, "Spare the rod and spoil the child."

In frontier regions, there were often no churches or resident ministers, but sometimes there were religious revivals, making profound if short-lived impressions on many children. And there were still hellfire-and-damnation preachers who terrified childish hearts with pronouncements like "Before the next Sabbath you may not only be taken sick, but taken away; and your tender bodies covered up in the cold and silent grave. . . ."

But the response was simply not what it used to be. Perhaps one reason for this was that the public schools, now proliferating rapidly, were not religiously oriented. Church and state being separate, no doctrine was taught in school, and some of the new school books scarcely mentioned the Deity.

The first Sunday school was founded in 1791 in Philadelphia by an Episcopal bishop who was tired of hearing children shouting outside his church during service. By the end of the Federal period, Sunday schools were a usual thing and only the strictly orthodox forced young children to attend long Sabbath services. There was also a flood of religious tracts, produced for a juvenile audience. In 1827 alone, 50,000 such tracts were printed and distributed for a penny or two each—or given away where

The things my parents bid me do,
Let me attentively pursue
The Good Boy's Soliloquy
(New York: Samuel Wood & Sons, 1822)

there were no pennies. The plots, which always involved goody-goodies and hardened little sinners, were unbelievable and the writing bad.

In a nation so ambitious for its children there was a great demand for juvenile books, and until about 1820 English writers were the ones who cashed in on it. Particularly popular were the cautionary verses of the English sisters Jane and Ann Taylor. A moral was attached to nearly all the poems, but they appealed to children because they dealt with familiar situations. Also, some of the bad children were permitted to reform and be forgiven. ("And never was he known again / Such naughty things to do.") Unlike the hapless youngsters in the German *Struvelpeter*, which dates from the same period, no child is hideously punished by burning up, poisoning, or falling under a cart.

The following Taylor poem, dealing with sibling rivalry, is as meaningful today as when it was published:

> O dear Mama, said little Fred
> Put baby down—take me instead
> Upon the carpet let her be
> Put baby down and take up me.
>
> No that my dear I cannot do
> You know I used to carry you
> But you are now grown strong and stout
> And you can run and play about.
>
> When Fanny is as old as you
> No doubt but what she'll do so too
> And when she grows a little stronger
> I mean to carry her no longer.

The Taylor poems were widely imitated, but the originals were the best. Another favorite English writer who set a trend was Mrs. Barbauld. She used simple language at a time when most writers for children made no concessions at all to childish vocabularies. One of her books, intended for very small children, offers large type, a few words to a page, and deals with an entirely uneventful day in the life of a small boy named Charles:

> Sop your bread in the tea.
> Pour the tea into the saucer. . . .
> Pull off his frock and petticoat
> Put on his nightcap.
> Lay his little head upon the pillow.
> Good night
> Shut your eyes.
> Go to sleep.

All rather prosaic, but easily comprehended by the very young, who had no other books. Charles Lamb objected to Mrs. Barbauld's works strenuously, saying, "Science has succeeded to poetry no less in the little walks of children than of men." But children liked it, probably because the little boy Charles was engaged in the very things that occupied the reader every day as well. Certainly it was more agreeable reading than most juvenile books of the day, which, in their enthusiasm for pressing a moral, often left the reader sad, guilt-ridden, and anxious. *My Mother's Grave*, an American effort printed in 1830, was very popular— popular, at least, with the parents who bought it. It told the story of a little girl who refused to bring her sick mother a glass of water. During the night the child repented, but when she went to apologize and make amends, she found that her mother had died. The book ends with a picture of the grave, and the words, "Oh! then, dear children, do not disoblige a parent, on any occasion, for fear you may, like the person above, regret it throughout all your life."

American writers also tried producing factual material for children. Unfortunately, they seemed to feel that facts were not quite respectable unless interwoven with religion. Here is a passage from a *Natural History*, published in Philadelphia in 1808:

PUPIL: Why is the firmament blue and the produce of the earth green?

TUTOR: In this appears the divine care for our welfare. These two soft, pleasing colours are agreeable to the eye . . . and neither weary nor injure the sight as some other colours do.

PUPIL: How many sorts of metals are there?

TUTOR: Six: gold, silver, copper, tin, lead, and iron.

PUPIL: What other valuable things are to be found in the earth's grand magazine?

TUTOR: That valuable fuel for fire—coals.

PUPIL: When such a vast quantity of this fuel is consumed every day, how great must be the store, which our kind Creator has made for our use!

This was not a school book. It was intended to be read at home, and to entertain as well as to instruct. "Fireside education" was recommended to mothers, who were urged to remember how Mrs. Washington had taught little George at her knee.

The early nineteenth century was a period of strenuous efforts to establish a good public school system—not an easy task in a country where children worked and the population was chiefly rural. Well-to-do city parents often objected to sending their children to public schools, for fear of corrupting influences. Besides that, school was often a grueling experience: hard benches, long hours, bad-tempered or cruel schoolmasters. "Torture rather than instruction" was what children often encountered in school, wrote Theodore Dwight, a Congressman, clergyman, and leading editor; and he added a pronouncement that is still valid: "School is a shock from which many bright children never recover."

Even the poorest parents, whose children needed free education most, seem to have been suspicious of it and slow to take advantage of it. A pamphlet circulated in 1828 in New York warned parents not to neglect their children's schooling: "They will live disgraced and when they die, go to the judgment seat of heaven in all the pollution of their sins." And all because their parents had failed in their duty. "Will you not have a most solemn and awful account to render to your God?" Frequent excuses were that the child had not the proper clothes, that he was needed at home, that he was sent out to collect chips, or that he refused to go. If the latter was the case, "take him to the police officer and pray for the privilege of his admission into the school for Juvenile Delinquents." For children over fourteen, the pamphleteer recommended an apprenticeship or "course of useful labor." And he reiterated the theme that all Americans knew and heard constantly and probably dreamed of: "In our free government the children of the poorest may rise to the highest station of wealth, honor, trust, and usefulness."

Among those who could afford it, private tutors were usually preferred to the turmoil of the public schoolhouse. One of the most intensive private educations of the day was given Theodosia Burr, the daughter of Aaron Burr, during the 1790s. (The education of daughters was one of the few subjects upon which Aaron Burr and Thomas Jefferson agreed; each plied their daughters with lessons.)

Theodosia's schedule, at age nine, called for "cipher" from five to eight in the morning and again from five to eight in the evening. French took two to three hours a day, and the little girl also studied Latin, Greek, and the harp. Her father, who was often away from home, wrote frequently to scold or praise her.

> Four pages in Lucian was a great lesson; and why, my dear Theo, can't this be done a little oftener? You must by this time, I think have gone through Lucian. I wish you to begin and go through again. . . . You say nothing of writing or learning Greek verbs;—is this practice discontinued? and why? . . . Do you

continue to preserve Madame de S's good opinion of your talents for the harp? . . . Some English or French history must employ a little of every day. . . . You may allot an hour for your journal. . . .

Burr takes his child to task for bad posture: "The continuance in this vile habit will certainly produce a consumption." And for faulty letter writing: "Arrange a whole sentence in your mind before you write a word of it; and whatever may be your 'hurry' (never be in a *hurry*), read over your letter slowly and carefully before you send it."

Letter writing was considered an important accomplishment in those days, but there is surely something in Burr's urgent instructions that goes beyond a desire to have his daughter accomplished. "Go on, my dear girl, and you will become all that I wish." It is the voice of the typical American parent, who longs for his children to succeed, to triumph, to reach ever greater heights.

Theodosia was the perfect daughter. Besides her scholastic attainments, she played the harp and piano, rode, and danced. From babyhood she slept alone in the dark and was trained to have "no fears, no nerves, no emotions, no self-indulgence." At her father's Greenwich Village house (then two miles north of New York City) she acted as hostess, her mother being dead, and, at fourteen, is described as discoursing to a large circle of ladies and gentlemen on the theories of Jeremy Bentham. Alas for all this effort and attainment: Theodosia perished at sea while still in her twenties.

Average American children never achieved such scholarship or savoir faire, but it was a usual custom to stuff a bright child with learning, whether the child was receptive or not. Theodosia Burr was apparently a willing student. Children who were unwilling often had a hard time of it, for it was part of the job of

73

a conscientious schoolmaster or mistress to mete out punishments that would not be forgotten. A birching on the posterior or hands was the most usual method, but some teachers were more inventive. One schoolmaster, in the South, made a point of beating every new boy until he either fainted or vomited. Another cracked a ruler on the children's hands so that they became too swollen and painful to use for days afterward. Boxing the ears was common and not infrequently caused lifelong deafness.

In 1829, a case involving an unwilling scholar and a zealous teacher, a clergyman named Samuel Arnold, came before the grand jury in New Hampshire. In his own behalf, the Reverend Arnold published a book called *An Astonishing Affair*, in which he gave the whole story from his own point of view.

Out of the goodness of his heart (Arnold wrote), he had taken Almon, the four-year-old son of a poor widow, into his house in order to teach him. One January morning, Arnold asked his student to spell and pronounce "gut-ter," a word he had spelled before; but, out of sheer contrariness, Almon refused to do so.

"You shall obey, or I will whip you till you do," announced the clergyman. The boy, he added, knew that Arnold always kept his word, for he had been punished before—not severely, but by being shut up in the (unheated) cellar, or by having his ears boxed—"not more than three or four times and lightly." Or, as a cure for lying, by being buttoned into his clothes, which he could not unbutton, for many hours—"nature pressing her demands and his troubles increasing."

But Almon remained contrary. "I snapt his ears repeatedly and used various mild measures to obtain obedience," Arnold wrote. "I know there are some who are not frightened at the consequences of an unsubdued will; but I am not of their number." He took the child into the cellar and stripped him. "It was very natural to take the child aside a little from the family

74

Sewing a fine seam
The Snow-Drop (New Haven: S. Babcock, ca. 1820)

and the cellar was light and perhaps as comfortable as any other apartment in the house where fire was not kept." He proceeded to beat him with birch tops, each as long as an arm and as sharp and flexible as a knitting needle. "With my wife present, I commenced using the rod according to Proverbs xxiii, 14th, 'thou shalt beat him with the rod, and shalt deliver his soul from hell.' I chastened him while there was hope, according to chapter 19, verse 10—'Chasten thy son while there is hope.' . . . I felt all the force of divine authority and express command. . . . It was better to break his will than to break my word."

But Almon "saw the sticks giving out" and insisted he could not spell *gutter*. When the birch rods broke, Arnold took up a crooked rough beechstick and the beating continued for "half or

75

three-quarters of an hour." As the beechstick refused to wear out, Almon finally "was subdued." It is not clear from Arnold's account whether he ever spelled the word, but he was "unusually mild, submissive, pleasant and interesting," ate a good dinner, and said, "I never had anybody so kind to me as you are." He died a few days later.

The Arnold case was widely reported in the newspapers and the outrage it engendered was probably symptomatic of a gentling of attitude toward children, just dawning in the Federal period. As we have seen, the Puritans deplored an idle child. Other denominations were slightly more lenient, but as late as 1785 an Episcopal catechism told boys and girls, "Let thy Recreation be Lawful, Brief, and Seldom." But by 1825 there were not only numerous American-written books for the amusement of children, but even one that described children's games and how to play them. Its authors were clearly nervous about it, for they wrote, "We would wish it to be understood that we are far, very far, from being willing to encourage more [play] of any kind." Their book, they assured parents, was intended "simply and alone to unbend the mind, and invigorate the body that [children] may again return to their studies or other useful employments with fresh energy and vigor."

Even in Boston there were now public entertainments to lure children: the Waxworks, for instance, where infant patriotism might be encouraged by the sight of a wax John Adams. In 1797, Boston children swarmed to see an elephant. Any elephant was unusual in Boston, but this one uncorked and drank thirty bottles of porter every day. (A generation later, when every city had its Temperance Society, such an animal would not have been considered a suitable spectacle for children.)

In 1822, Clement Moore wrote *A Visit from St. Nicholas*, thus helping to spread the fame of the Dutch Christmas saint far beyond the confines of New York. Fourth of July had become a stimulating occasion for children. They were encouraged to compose and deliver orations and every town and village had its Fourth of July parade, wherein veterans of the Revolution marched and young girls dressed as goddesses of Liberty rode in "triumphal chariots." Picnics and fireworks made a heady and exciting day in young lives geared to steady work and almost no excitement at all.

Book learning was still a small and rather unimportant part of what was understood to be meant by the word *education*. According to *The Parent's Monitor and Young People's Friend*, one of the many parents' magazines that began to appear after 1830, education meant "the implanting of right dispositions, the cultivation of the heart, the guidance of the temper, the formation of character." It was not for a generation or two later that the word *education* came to mean primarily what one learned in school. In a little book called *A Pretty New Year's Gift*, published in Worcester in 1796, the word was a synonym for *upbringing;* and the following sentence, though somewhat awkwardly phrased, might serve as a reminder to all parents, anywhere in time or place:

> There is nothing where people are so very wrong as in the education of children, though there is nothing in which they ought to be more absolutely certain of being right.

Topsy bringing flowers to Eva
Pictures and Stories from Uncle Tom's Cabin, 1853

4

CHILDREN OF THE ANTEBELLUM SOUTH

"Why mustn't I spin and churn, Millie?"
"Ladies don't nuvver do dem things."
"Then why can I help with the laces and muslins?"
"Cause—ladies *does* do dem things."
My Day, by Mrs. Roger Pryor (1909)

YEARS LATER, THE DAUGHTER OF AN ANTEBELLUM PLANTER remembered this conversation, which had taken place between herself as a small child and her black mammy. In retrospect life in the Old South seemed to her to have been an unalloyed delight—not only for her but for Mammy too and for everyone else on the plantation.

For a long time after the Civil War, memoirs were published by men and women who had grown up in the "big houses" of antebellum plantations and who, all their lives, had carried around a sense of having been thrown out of Paradise. (Some of those "big houses" were unpretentious farmhouses, but nostalgia plays tricks with the memory.)

"I believed the world one vast plantation bounded by negro

79

quarters," wrote Letitia M. Burwell in *A Girl's Life in Virginia*; and "no young princesses could have received from admiring subjects more adulation" than herself and her sisters from the slaves around them. Slaves were not called slaves, of course. They were servants. "We had never heard the word 'slave.' " And she was certain that all on her father's plantation were treated kindly. Slave traders (known as "speculators") were a horror not to be mentioned, and unkind masters were socially ostracized.

In Mississippi, three little girls nicknamed Diddy, Dumps, and Tot lived a similar enchanted life. (Dumps later wrote about it.) Their handsome papa brought them dolls and books from New Orleans on the steamboat. They had a pet lamb and a pony and they played hide-and-seek and lady-come-to-see. Sometimes "little nigs" from the Quarters were fetched to play with them; or they went with Mammy to the Quarters to watch the "nigs" say their prayers and take their vermifuge. At Christmas there were presents for everyone, black and white, and once there was a slave wedding in the big house, with the bride in a white dress and veil and the ceremony performed by an illiterate old black preacher. Massa gave the bride away. (Slave marriages had no legal validity, of course, but Diddy, Dumps, and Tot knew nothing of that.)

One time a "speculator" camped in the neighborhood with a gang of slaves for sale. As Dumps remembered it, "the great majority looked exceedingly happy," well-fed and well-clothed. The speculator was a jolly fat man. Well, yes, perhaps a few were sad, especially one woman, nearly white, who was sick, and fearful for her child. "Her devotion to her baby was unusual in a slave." Papa bought this woman, who had been brought up almost as a daughter, though a slave, by a Maryland family and had married a white man. When he died, she and her baby had been sold "down the river." One of Papa's old slaves, Uncle Bob, gave his savings to send her and her child to New York. Except for this incident, nothing ruffled the serene progress of life at this plantation—until the war. Then Papa joined the army and was killed in battle, the house was burned, and the children's mother went insane. Tot died young, Diddy was early widowed, and Dumps ended as a schoolteacher.

It was always other people who were unkind to their slaves—people who never wrote their memoirs. An old gentleman who had been raised on a Carolina plantation wrote, "Nowhere in America was slavery a gentler, kindlier thing than in the Carolina low country." On his fifth birthday, he had been given a pony, a fowling piece, and a black "play-child" whose duty it was to both serve and play with him.

A "play-child" was a widespread institution, although some white families believed that their children would be corrupted by such an association and punished both black and white children if they were caught playing together. "I was never tyrannical," reminisced the Carolina gentleman, "as southern boys generally were not, but sometimes a little positive and threatening. . . ."

Fortunately, we are able to get some idea of the play-child's viewpoint through a series of interviews with old slaves, made in the 1930s as a WPA project. One aged man remembered how his white masters used to warm him at the fire until he was saturated with heat and then put him crossways at the bottom of the bed—to warm their feet. Another remembered being chosen as a play-child by the mistress, after a contest of running, jumping, walking on hands, and so on, among the Quarters children. The mistress said to him, "I give your young master over to you and if you let him hurt himself I'll pull your ears; if you let him cry I'll pull your ears, and if he wants anything and you don't let him have it, I'll pull your ears."

At the age of ten or eleven, a promising black girl might be brought into the house to be trained as a nursemaid or ladies' maid. She would comb little "Missy's" hair, fan her, bring her her slippers, and so on. One old woman recalled that the white babies were "mos'ly carried roun' on pillows till dey big 'nough to walk . . . wouldn't let 'em sit up till dey one year old." Jessie Benton Frémont, raised on her grandfather's plantation, recalled that she had not been allowed to use a poker, for fear she might "spread her hand."

Southern antebellum whites, although as scrupulously modest as any other Victorians, did not always apply the same standards to their black servants. One ex-slave said that until he was fully grown he wore only a one-piece smock with nothing under it, which he found embarrassing when called upon to run or jump. Visitors from Europe or the North were sometimes shocked in southern households to find themselves being waited on at table by nearly naked boys.

Josiah Quincy, of Boston, received another kind of shock. "It is far from being uncommon," he wrote, "to see a gentleman at dinner and his reputed offspring a slave to the master of the table. I myself saw two instances of this and the company very facetiously would trace the lines, linements and features of the father and mother in the child and very accurately point out the more characteristic resemblance. The fathers, neither of them blushed or seemed disconcerted. They were called men of worth, politeness and humanity."

A southern woman, Mrs. Mary Chesnut, wrote in her diary, "God forgive us, but ours is a monstrous system. . . . Like the patriarchs of old, our men live all in one house with their wives and their concubines; and the mulattoes one sees in every family partly resemble the white children. Any lady is ready to tell you who is the father of all the mulatto children in everybody's household but her own. Those, she seems to think, drop from the clouds."

Mrs. Chesnut felt free to express herself on this subject within the covers of her private diary, but it was not a thing to be discussed in public. If Victorian women everywhere were supposed to guard their purity and delicacy and stay on their pedestals, in the South they were purer and more delicate and

Mistress and slave
The Slave's Friend, vols. 1 and 2, 1836

had farther to fall. A book called *A Father's Legacy to His Daughters*, by Dr. Gregory, an English clergyman, found an attentive audience in the South, where directions like these were taken very seriously:

> Though good health be one of the greatest blessings of life . . . enjoy it in grateful silence. We men so naturally associate the idea of female softness and delicacy with a correspondent delicacy of constitution that when a woman speaks of her great strength, her extraordinary appetite, her ability to bear excessive fatigue, we recoil at the description, in a way she is little aware of.

And yet the wife of a planter worked very hard, overseeing a large household and a whole village of slaves. If she were a conscientious woman, she was busy from morning to night nursing, teaching, keeping household accounts, and supervising every domestic task. Letitia Burwell wrote that no one on the plantation seemed to have a care "except my mother."

But how did girls who were brought up to do nothing and know nothing become so full of purpose and efficiency as soon as they were married? Apparently the trick was to learn without seeming to learn. In Charleston, the Grimké sisters were required by their father to learn to spin and weave, shell corn, and pick cotton. But—as they later pointed out (they grew up to become abolitionists)—they knew they would never have to do it and so it was more or less of a game. Many girls never did learn, and plantation houses were often badly and extravagantly run. One of our memoirists grew up in a household that was entirely managed—and well managed—by Mammy Grace and Uncle Mandelbert. Another remembered that when she was a bride, at the age of sixteen, she knew nothing about housekeeping so simply left it all to the slaves until she got older.

If there was a stereotype that southern girls had to live up to, there was one for boys that was even more exacting. The young heir of Somerset Place, in North Carolina, is described as the personification of this ideal: he was "handsome, lavish, gentle as a girl, gay as a bird, chivalrous as any plumed knight, strong, brave to rashness, the best horseman, the deadliest shot, the fleetest skater, the greatest beau, the strongest man, the finest boxer, and the most eloquent speaker. . . ." He was also "autocratic as the czar," but, "when unopposed, the soul of courtesy, amiability and kindness."

Thomas Jefferson once offered the following comparison between northerners and southerners. In the North, he said, people are cool, sober, laborious, independent, jealous of their own liberties and just to those of others, interested, chicaning, and superstitious and hypocritical in their religion. Whereas in the South, they are fiery, voluptuary, indolent, unsteady, zealous for their own liberties but trampling on those of others, generous, candid, and without attachment or pretensions to any religion but that of the heart. Whether or not Jefferson was right in every particular of his list, he rightly discerned that the two major sections of the United States were very different. Identifying the segments of southern society, he said that there were aristocrats, descendants and relatives of aristocrats, the newly rich, whom he called "pretenders," independent yeomen, and overseers. Others have named just three classes: the planters (a small minority), the middling sort, and the poorer sort.

The middling sort included the merchants, skilled artisans, and professional people of the towns, and farmers who were well enough off to keep a few slaves. The poorer sort were in the majority and most of them were upcountry farmers who managed a subsistence living. An education was hard for them to come by, but if they were lucky there might be a field school in their vicinity or a literate neighbor willing to teach children.

An Englishman traveling in the South soon after the Revolution said that the two lower classes were very ignorant. The men he found to be savage and brutal, but the women, "benevolent, humane, amiable and kind. . . . [They] excel the men, beyond comparison." He fell half in love with a fifteen-year-old backwoods girl named Betsy. In her he saw "a degree of generosity, sentiment and the most delicate sensibility that very few of the more polished and accomplished ladies can boast of. . . . She endeavored to please and she gave delight." But, of course, being a gentleman, he could not consider marrying Betsy and he left her in the backwoods and returned to England.

Dancing seems to have been taught, even when nothing else was. A traveler in the Blue Ridge Mountains about 1800 found a dancing master ensconced at a country tavern. Parents brought their boys and girls to him from great distances for weekly lessons in the minuet, reels, and country dances. The little girls, the traveler called "pretty little modern-dressed misses, dressed and ornamented to a ridiculous pitch of extravagance." This same observer found that the children of "the vulgar" enjoyed far too much freedom. He saw well-dressed youths shouting and swearing on the streets of towns, drinking in taverns, and smoking cigars. In Alexandria he was appalled to see a four-year-old puffing on a large cigar. "The infatuated father," who was a cigar maker, said the child smoked three or four or more daily "or he would cry for them" or "would steal them when opportunity offered."

Education, for both boys and girls in the South, was sometimes good and sometimes very poor, depending on how interested the parents were. Robert E. Lee attended a school maintained at one of the Carter plantations for Carter children and their cousins (Lee's mother was a Carter). This enabled him to get into West Point without difficulty. His aunt, Mrs. Randolph, who had a lot to do with his upbringing, said her principle in child raising was "whip and pray and pray and whip." Some planters employed a northern or an English governess or tutor to teach their children. Parents who could not afford that might send their children to small boarding schools in New Orleans, Charleston, or New York. Female education was usually limited to dancing, music, French, and sketching, and anything more was, according to one memoirist, "considered queer." If a little girl learned Latin and Greek with her brothers, she kept it quiet. However, southern ladies were often widely read in good literature. Mrs. Chesnut, for example, read Schiller and Goethe, Dumas and Hugo in the original.

Brilliant and erratic John Randolph preceded his many years in Congress with a childhood running wild. He seems to have had some schooling when his parents happened to think of it, and at fifteen was sent to Columbia. "I am an ignorant man, sir," he was prone to say. Yet he was widely read and a talented orator.

The Massachusetts writer Thomas Higginson had this to say about his southern classmates at Harvard during the late 1830s: "Charming manners, social aptitudes, imperious ways, abundant leisure, and plenty of money." Some were brilliant and went on to Harvard Law School. Others were grossly ignorant. One had to be taught to read and write before he could attend classes. "On the other hand, they were often indolent, profligate, and quarrelsome; and they were almost wholly responsible for the 'town and gown' quarrels, now extinct, but then not infrequent."

Southern boys may have found southern colleges more to their liking. One fifteen-year-old, J. Motte Alston, who went to St. Mary's College in Baltimore was allowed by the president to sleep late and to go into the city to visit his "lady friends, who, by the way, sometimes came to see me. . . ." Alston describes what a fifteen-year-old college man wore: black trousers and vest, a dress coat of dark blue broadcloth with wrought buttons, a silk hat, and a stock made of horsehair covered with silk (the horsehair was scratchy and was meant to encourage the wearer to keep his head well up).

At Franklin College in Athens, Georgia, the president complained that most of the students spent more of their time shooting, dueling, drinking, and gambling than on their lessons. Since few of them were preparing for a profession, they were only marking time until they should return to their farms and plantations.

One child in Mississippi, poor but proud, the youngest of ten children, went to a field school and then told his father he had had enough of education. His father said to him, "It is for you to elect whether you will work with your head or your hands—but you must work." After a day of cotton picking, he decided he liked school after all. This boy later went to West Point, where he was graduated in 1828.

His name? Jefferson Davis.

A visit from St. Nicholas
Courtesy of F.A.O. Schwarz, New York

5

CHRISTIAN NURTURE

"WHAT A SACRED OFFICE IS THAT OF THE PARENT!"
exclaimed an anonymous contributor to *The Parent's Magazine* in
December, 1840. He predicted that by 1915 the population of the
United States would reach 156,000,000 (actually it reached only
about 100,000,000), and "what an influence when [the parent]
may mould the character of that distant day and of that
multitudinous population! . . . What destiny temporal and
eternal awaits it depends upon parents now upon the stage. . . .
An individual is now something; he is known and felt, and claims
his influence and importance; then individuality will almost be
lost when the greatest man is only one in *one hundred and fifty-six
million!*"

Need he have distressed himself? Even in a population of
over two hundred million, the average American feels himself to
be "something" and "claims his influence and importance"—
perhaps rather too much so at times. Just as the *Parent's*
contributor predicted, those mothers and fathers who were "upon

the stage" in 1840 did indeed have a far-reaching influence. Hardly anyone remembers it now and it was scarcely apparent then, but the parents of that generation were the pioneers of permissive child rearing.

In our time the name of Dr. Benjamin Spock comes to mind when permissiveness is mentioned. But in fact, in the middle and late nineteenth century, there were dozens of writers on child care who could match him and several who wildly outdid him. The latter were at the farthest swing of a pendulum that had moved from an opposite extreme, the rigidity of Puritanism.

Traditional child-rearing methods were not abandoned easily, but by 1830 changes were clearly on the way. The Republic was young and rambunctious. It had achieved its independence not through submission and a broken will but through self-assertion—a lesson not lost on bright children, who were urged to be patriotic and to learn their country's history. "In every home in our land, the altar of patriotism should stand beside the altar of religion," was the pronouncement of one writer on child care. "Mothers should teach the first lesson in history in one word—Washington."

Note that *mothers* are specified, not fathers. With the progress of the new industrial age, fathers were likely to be away from home for ten or more hours a day, six days a week. They necessarily delegated the reins of child management to their wives, who were often young things in their teens or early twenties—eager and determined but woefully uncertain, and suspecting that the changing times required changed methods. In 1830, a mother looking for a book on child care would have found that the few that were available gave far more attention to physical care, manners, and salvation than to everyday problems of management. But in only a few years the situation was entirely changed: a mother would scarcely have found time to read all the advice available. She could learn what to do if her little boy should bite the baby (bite him back); whether to tell a child to believe in ghosts (yes, because there are supernatural beings in the Bible and children must believe the Bible); and how to administer punishment. Dr. John Abbott, author of the most popular child-care book of the 1830s, *The Mother at Home*, was not opposed to beating, but advised against shutting children up in dark closets or cellars. While insisting on a child's absolute obedience and total submission of will, he warned parents not to punish for accidents or ignorance and not to pepper children with continual commands. If a whipping became inevitable, a mother should remain cool while making sure to inflict real pain. "It makes mother very unhappy to have to punish you," she should say, adding, when the child appeared contrite, "Do you wish me to ask God to forgive you?" (for it must be clear that a parent acted as the Lord's surrogate).

Theodore Dwight, in *The Father's Book* (1834)—despite the title, the book was also for mothers—showed sympathy and tenderness for small children, even while subscribing to the Calvinist doctrine that their natures are inherently evil ("The nature of man is ever running one way."). He enjoined parents to soothe and divert fretful little ones and thus avoid confrontations. Further, he recognized that children should not be blamed or punished for behaving like children. He suggested that fathers ask themselves a question that seems as valid now as it was then: "What is my business and ought it to engross me so as to make me a stranger to my children?"

Abbott and Dwight tempered their Calvinism with compassion, but the old orthodox views of child rearing died hard. The mothers' magazines that proliferated during the 1830s and '40s took for granted that a certain awe-inspiring implement, the rod (usually either a slender switch of birch or apple or a whalebone from Mamma's stays), was kept in a handy and conspicuous place in all households. Theoretically, it would be seldom needed if the parents did an efficient job of subduing their children, preferably at the first sign of defiance. ". . . They go astray as soon as they be born, speaking lies," said the psalmist. With this in mind, there were parents who whipped nursing babies on the ground that the little wretches were thinking and acting lies, even though too young to enunciate them—plotting ways of getting attention, for instance, by feigning hunger or pain. Lying was one of the worst of sins and practically guaranteed the liar an eternity spent in "the lake which burneth with fire and brimstone." One seven-year-old who told his father a lie in order to cover up a forbidden skating expedition pined away and died of remorse—even though he confessed the lie ten minutes after telling it and was at once suitably corrected with the rod.

A *Mothers* magazine of 1833 told of a sixteen-month-old baby girl who was able to say "dear Mamma," but one day declined to do so on command.

"Say, 'dear Mamma,' " insisted dear Mamma.

"Won't," replied the child, and the battle was joined. For four hours the mother alternately whipped her daughter and shut her in the closet. At last "dear Mamma" was forthcoming and the Devil exorcised. Whether he ever attempted a comeback in this case is not recorded, but as late as 1858 we read a description of an infant boy whose will was broken at ten months. He was taught "never even to cry in his father's presence," and when he grew up his chief delight was in rendering his parents happy; their wish was his law. "Life to such a child is never a burden," wrote his chronicler, the Reverend Orange Clark. "A parent's will to him is paramount, and cheerfulness and happy industry crown his days."

Although the young American mother of the 1830s may have been confused by conflicting advice, she threw herself into her new role as energetically as her husband threw himself into his business. Her most important job, everyone told her, was to produce sons who would become the nation's leaders and who would someday say, like George Washington, "Home influence directed by a pious mother is the source of my success." As for the daughters, they were to become gentle, devout, high-principled, and accomplished—not so much in domestic skills as in such pursuits as piano playing, embroidery, and reading Sir Walter Scott aloud and with expression. The old-fashioned domestic skills, such as spinning, weaving, and making candles, were no longer esteemed. Some mothers did not even teach their girls to cook and dust. In the first place it was now possible to buy many necessities ready-made and to hire immigrant Irish girls to do the dirty work, and in the second the American middle class was slowly becoming infected by the Old World idea that ladies and gentlemen did not work with their hands. Better travel facilities now enabled rich Americans to visit England and the Continent, whence they were likely to return (as the New York diarist Philip Hone complained) full of "the foppery of foreign manners and the bad taste of anti-Americanism." Their less prosperous but upwardly mobile neighbors watched what they did and tried to imitate them.

Old-fashioned people railed against the bad influence of un-American notions. Mrs. Lydia Child argued in *The Mother's Book* (1844) that daughters must be prepared to fill any station in life: ". . . half our people are in a totally different situation from what might have been expected in their childhood." In case a girl's fate took her downward, she should be able to support herself; if she moved up, domestic efficiency should be no disgrace. Mrs. Child pointed out that Abigail Adams, "the admiration of European courts . . . knew how to make butter and cheese as well as any woman in Weymouth."

Foreign observers were almost always dismayed by American children, finding them precocious, noisy, and disrespectful of their elders. One of the more charitable critics, the German Francis J. Grund, thought that the phenomenon was caused by bad climate, long school hours (a boy between four and six years old was likely to spend six hours a day in school and three more doing homework), and the fact that American parents "live altogether for their children." Harriet Martineau also noted this devotion and added shrewdly that it was natural for children to occupy an important place in a country of enormous resources and small population.

Other foreign visitors were less polite. "Baby citizens are allowed to run wild as the Snake Indians and do whatever they please," was one comment. As for young girls, according to the English traveler Mrs. Baxter, they had "nothing to recommend them but thoughtlessness and volubility." They "acquire at an early age a self-confidence and a freedom of demeanour by no means feminine," and, furthermore, they flirt, lounge, read novels, and do not help their mothers. Another visitor from England, William Fergusson, remarked, "There are no children in our sense of the term in America—only little men and women. . . . The merest boy will give his opinion upon the subject of conversation among his seniors; and he expects to be listened to, and is."

There was hardly a dissenting voice in this chorus of complaint. Charles Dickens reserved some of his most masterfully caustic remarks for American small fry who crossed his path. And another visitor, Lady Emmeline Wortley, whose comments were ordinarily gentle and complimentary, felt obliged to say, "The one point, perhaps, in which I most concur with other writers on the United States is there being no real childlike children here. . . . A 'dreadful bright boy' will tell you perchance, with his tiny squeaking voice, 'we air a great people, by thunder, the greatest on the airth, and can do all things double first-rate.' . . ."

Yet never before in history had there been children so worried over and thought about as those little Americans born in the second quarter of the nineteenth century. And judging by the memoirs and autobiographies that a number of them later wrote, happy childhoods were not uncommon.

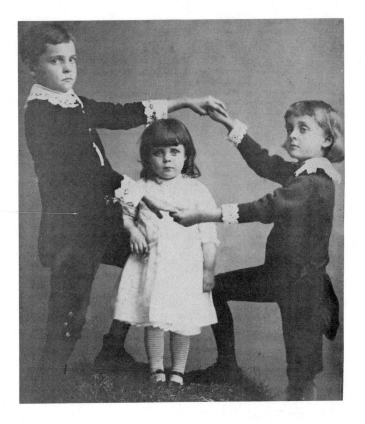

The rising generation
Collection of the author

Backward, turn backward, O Time, in your flight,
Make me a child again just for tonight!

These are the opening lines of "Rock Me to Sleep," one of the most popular poems of the nineteenth century. It was learned by heart, wept over, recited in elocution classes, and given at Christmas in a keepsake edition bound in blue and gold. Its

95

author, Mrs. Elizabeth Akers Allen, was born in 1832, a member of the generation in which children began so noticeably to assert themselves. If the response to "Rock Me to Sleep" is any criterion, many of Mrs. Allen's contemporaries also treasured childhood memories. For example, Julian Hawthorne, in his autobiography, wrote that if angels had given him permission to choose his own fate, he would have answered, "Let me be the only son of Nathaniel Hawthorne and his wife Sophia, born in Boston, Massachusetts, at 1 o'clock in the morning of June 22nd, in the year 1846"—which is just what he was. Lucy Larcom, born in 1824, was one of ten children of a family so poor that when the father died, the little girls had to go to work in the Lowell mills. Nevertheless, she remembers her childhood as a joyful one. "We were a neighborhood of large families, and most of us enjoyed the privilege of a little wholesome neglect. Our tether was a long one. . . ." And ". . . the happiness of our lives was rooted in the stern, vigorous virtues of the people we lived among. . . . There was granite in their character and beliefs, but it was granite that could smile in the sunshine and clothe itself with flowers. We little ones felt the firm rock beneath us and were lifted up on it, to emulate their goodness and to share their aspirations." (We, of the anxious, peripatetic twentieth century, have our own name for that kind of granite and sunshine: security.)

One could go on at length with these glimpses of satisfactory childhoods. Nevertheless, there were definite drawbacks to child life of that time, and most of us would find them hard to bear. Schools were stuffy and uncomfortable, the hours long, the masters handy with the rod. Children's clothing inhibited play. Medications were horrid (for headache, leeches sucking blood at the back of the neck; for stomachache, a sticky paste of rhubarb and magnesia; for almost anything, castor oil). But worst of all, about a third of the children born did not live past the age of five.

This was better than the "more than half" of colonial times, but it was still appalling. Tuberculosis took a terrible toll of adolescents and puerperal fever of mothers. This high mortality rate was nothing new, of course, but now the widening horizons of science and the decline of Puritanism made meek resignation more difficult. The doctrine of infant damnation was becoming very unpopular.

But if there was a falling off in heartfelt devotion to Calvinism, there was little slackening of outward religious observance. "Remember the sabbath day, to keep it holy" was as important a Commandment for most Americans as the seventh or the sixth. In most homes no work or play was permitted on the Sabbath, and the close of that day brought Bible reading and hymn singing. "What can be more delightful on earth," asked Theodore Dwight in *The Father's Book,* "than the Sabbath in a family where every arrangement and practice has been established in conformity with the principles of the gospel?" Yet Dr. Dwight allowed a few un-Puritan laxities that disturbed the orthodox. He thought that *small* children might be given a toy or two on the Sabbath and that since pews are uncomfortable for little people—their feet dangle—they might be allowed sometimes to stand up on the seat and look about. Kind parental looks and even a few sugarplums might also help them through the service. However, there could be no question of leaving them at home or sending them to Sunday school instead.

A Boston Brahmin lady, born in 1842, writes of a contented childhood—except for Sunday. "Sunday," she states flatly, "was a dreadful day." On the other hand, Thomas Wentworth Higginson, born some years earlier into the same milieu, remembers "mild" Sundays. His mother circumvented the prohibition of secular music on the Sabbath by decreeing that "all good music is sacred." Higginson even notes in his memoirs a Sunday afternoon when he actually played ball behind the barn. Apparently, Mrs. Higginson did not subscribe to *Mothers* maga-

97

zine; if she had, she might have been dismayed by the story of a condemned murderer who said, "When I was quite young, I had many stings of conscience, till one Sabbath I went into a neighbor's cornfield and plucked three ears of corn *and my mother boiled them for me.* From that fatal hour my career of sin and impiety has been unbroken till it has at length brought me to the gallows." Deploring the laxity of the times, *Mothers* went on to say that in the old days a child who played in church would find the minister stopping the sermon to bellow out his name and command him to report to the parsonage the next day. But now (1833), ministers seemed to have lost their power to terrify (*Mothers*, it might be noted, was edited by ministers). And if they preached the doctrine of infant damnation, the result was likely to be newly empty seats in the meetinghouse rather than new conversions.

There was no doubt that the sterner Protestant communions—the Congregationalists, Presbyterians, Dutch Reformeds, and Lutherans—were losing members to the Unitarians and Episcopalians (the latter being the American offshoot of the Church of England). To the rescue, in 1842, came a Congregationalist minister named Horace Bushnell. He relieved the minds of thousands by pointing the way to reconciliation between the old beliefs and the new. In his book *Christian Nurture,* Bushnell postulated that children are not born depraved but are "formless lumps" at birth, equally capable of good or of evil. If the parent gives proper guidance ("Christian nurture"), the child will grow and thrive in goodness. Religion should not be presented as a gloomy restraint but as "the friend of play." Children should not be scolded for inattention in church, nor should they be "worried and drummed into apathy by dogmatic catechisms." While parents "personate God in the child's feelings and conscience," they must be careful how they use their authority. If they are harsh and rejecting, the child will feel shut out from God.

Although Bushnell's book was primarily intended to present a religious doctrine, it was filled with helpful hints on the daily management of children. Some of them seem to foretell modern psychology. Bushnell was the only writer of his day to suggest that children pass through developmental stages. An infant, he said, is at the "stage of impressions"; the first three years are of more importance in character building than any "stage" that follows. The young absorb the faults and virtues of their parents, who must therefore make an enormous effort to be wise and self-controlled. While parents must not be harsh, neither must they be overprotective, for then the child will grow up lacking in self-confidence. The trick is to slowly let him go so that he will be able to stand on his own as an adult; not to break his will but to teach him to control it.

Bushnell's superiors in the Congregational church were not ready for *Christian Nurture*. In fact, they found it so distressing that Bushnell withdrew it from circulation. But he went on preaching, and twenty years later, when his ideas no longer seemed radical, he revised and reissued the book and it became a best seller. By the time of his death in 1878, most clergymen and most child-care writers found Bushnell's methods normal, if perhaps even a little old-fashioned.

By midcentury there had clearly been a revolution in child management, even though it took time for its impact to spread from the comparatively few parents who read books and magazines and were not afraid of new ideas. Some advice was reiterated for decades before it became common procedure. For example, we read again and again of the necessity for fresh air in the nursery; or of the therapeutic benefits of allowing little girls to dress simply so that they might romp and play; or of the ill effects of forcing children to show off their brilliance in front of mother's friends. America must have abounded with stuffy nurseries, wan little girls keeping their dresses clean, and shrill voices declaiming the Declaration of Independence.

During the latter half of the century, the flood of child-care advice continued unabated, growing slowly more secular and more permissive. In this it reflected the mood of a middle-class America that was changing its values. The shattering effects of the Civil War, the winning of the West, the movement to the cities, the declining power of the Protestant ethic, the rise of great wealth and great poverty, and the dawning awareness that millions of fellow Americans did not share Anglo-Saxon middle-class traditions (the idea that they might not *want* to share them was still far distant)—all these factors combined against a rigid society. A mother's impulse was to screen her little ones from this complicated world. Father would go out and cope with it, but it was too perplexing and sordid a place for mothers and children.

The self-appointed child experts still backed themselves up with scripture whenever appropriate, but now the favorite quotation was Saint Paul's "Provoke not your children to wrath." Some even advanced the theory that when Solomon had said, "Spare the rod and spoil the child," he had not meant that parents should actually lay hands on their children but that they should maintain discipline by wielding a *symbolic* rod. That might sound tricky, but if anyone could manage it, it would be "the gentle ruler," the "force that is to the moral world what the steam-engine is to the physical," she who is "one of God's own vice-regents," without whom "men cannot stir a step in life to purpose." In other words, "the Christian mother—ah, in her what influences center! From her what perfumes breathe, what dews distil, what forces, still but mighty, ever emanate!" (These are quotes from several late nineteenth-century essays on mother-hood.) By the 1870s there was a tacit understanding in most households that child management was the mother's province, by *right,* and not just because it suited Father.

Gentle Measures in the Management of the Young (1871) went through many editions until the end of the century. Its author, Jacob Abbott, had enormous prestige with mothers because for years he had been turning out the wholesome, moralistic, and boring *Rollo* books, as well as countless other stories and histories for the young. He was an ordained (but not practicing) minister, a schoolmaster, and the brother of John Abbott, who back in the thirties had written *The Mother at Home*. Abbott told the late-Victorian mother exactly what she wanted to hear: that hers was an exalted and difficult mission; that it was possible to be both gentle and authoritative at the same time; and that she need not feel guilty if she were, in certain areas, permissive. (He did not use that word; instead, his favorites were *gentle* and *unoppressive*.) Children, said Abbott, ought to be given "the greatest freedom of action. . . . It seems to me that children are not generally indulged enough . . . as a general rule, the more that children are gratified in respect to their childish fancies and impulses and even their caprices when no evil or danger is to be apprehended, the better." However, like good soldiers they must obey their parents implicitly, "even when they know their way is better or as good." The suggestion that a child might be capable of a better idea than his parents would have shocked oldtimers. About this time Emerson quoted a friend, a "witty physician," as having remarked that "it was a misfortune to have been born when children were nothing and to live till men were nothing."

But the pendulum had still not swung all the way. Some of the child-care books of the eighties and nineties made *Gentle Measures* look old-fashioned, arbitrary, and even cruel. ". . . abolish law or the appearance of law" was the message of one Mrs. Mattie W. Trippe in *Home Treatment for Children* (1881). "Let [the child] revel in an absolute sense of freedom, feeling only the restraints of affection." In the opinion of Mrs. F. McCready Harris in *Plain Talks with Young Homemakers* (1889), children should be permitted to slide down the banisters because they will probably do it anyway. "If you forbid them, in nine cases out of ten you teach them to deceive. Better coax them not to out of love and pity for you, who can not help feeling nervous, thus appealing to their chivalry; or . . . spread your pillows and blankets . . . and let them have a grand slide. Any trouble, any wear and tear of clothes and furniture, is better than risking our child being pushed to a lie."

Chivalry was much on the minds of late-Victorian parents. They had been raised on Tennyson, after all, and were prone to give their children early English names, such as Arthur, Maude, Ethel, and Egbert. *Making the Best of Our Children*, by Mary Wood-Allen, was published in 1909, but its ideas are those of the nineties. It demonstrated to mothers how chivalry might help build character. When little Franklin pushes his sister Lucy into the lake, their mother, Mrs. Dawson, says, "I've been wondering if we left my little Sir Arthur at home today." Franklin argues that Lucy deserved what she got, since she tore his hat and threw it in the water. But Mrs. Dawson points out that the business of a true knight is to fight for the weak and to succor distressed damsels ("Do you think Sir Arthur would have pushed a little girl into the water?"). Franklin at once becomes contrite, and when he sees his sister "shining in her clean attire," he kisses her and begs forgiveness. No rod ever enters the picture; the Dawsons probably do not own one.

In *The Science of Motherhood* (1894), Mrs. Hannah Whitall Smith advised mothers to *win* their children to goodness—"don't drive them." If a boy pounds nails into the furniture give him some blocks into which nails can be hammered; a little girl who cuts holes in the curtains or in her clothes should be supplied with colored paper to cut—and an explanation as to why. Mothers, give reasons—so that the child will learn to *choose* the right! Don't nag, be polite, and use the word "don't" as little as possible. "The will is one of the most sacred parts of our nature and should no more be broken than the main shaft of a steam-engine."

Elizabeth Glover's *Children's Wing* (1889) is a denunciation of the well-to-do for shunting the young off among nurses and servants. "Sensitive, delicate, little born ladies and gentlemen," she declared, "should not . . . keep uncultivated company. . . . Their fathers and mothers could not bear such companionship for an hour. . . . The child is born with all the sensibilities of the class to which it belongs." The author's solution to the problem was not that mothers should stay at home and mind the children but that the children should be taken about and invited to grown-up parties.

Probably not many children were indulged to the extent recommended in these books, but for the great majority of middle-class, native-born American children the norm was certainly a good deal of freedom, with family life providing an anchor and a sense of belonging. The world had not yet learned to thrust itself into families. Without TVs, radios, uncensored books and magazines, "R" movies, many telephones, and fast, easily available transportation, it was easy for parents to keep an eye on their children and still not seem oppressive. A child, said Kate Douglas Wiggin, the author of *Rebecca of Sunnybrook Farm*, "has a right to a genuine, free, serene, healthy, bread-and-butter childhood." She thought the best place for the young was a farm, where they could pick blueberries and slide down haystacks and feed chickens. The life of a farm was one in which "the child can share, and in the sharing of which he is moved to a sense of his own responsibilities." (But by 1900, half the population was living in cities.) The less a child had to do with adults and their concerns the better, lest he "miss his childhood."

In his autobiography, *The Age of Confidence*, Henry Seidel Canby tells of growing up in the nineties as a member of a prosperous family in a small city. His parents, he tells us, had a laissez-faire attitude toward their children. "Parents were by no means indulgent, yet they seemed usually to be secretly leagued with us to give the child a chance in the house. They let him alone unless he was outrageous. . . . It was the grandparents you had to watch out for." It was his opinion that homes of the nineties were happier than in the "previous generation," because they offered "more give and take between parents and children, more liberty and more cheerfulness." Mother was usually at home, meals appeared regularly, "our house moved with felt rhythms." Sunday was more a day of the family than a day of religion. "The parents left religion to the Church and the Church left it to the service and the Bible." (The Canbys attended the Episcopal church, although earlier generations had been Presbyterians and Quakers.) To attend church was a matter of course, but "there was a tacit understanding between the two younger generations that hellfire had been overdone, though of course no open acknowledgment. It seemed to be agreed that if we stuck to character, hellfire need not be expected."

Children of Canby's generation lived in a Golden Age as far as books were concerned. Some of the best literary talent in the English-speaking world was catering to their tastes. No more stories written solely to convey a moral, no more tedious and preachy histories, no more suppression of fairy stories. From England came the works of Lewis Carroll, George Macdonald, Edward Lear, Charlotte Yonge, and E. Nesbit. Thackeray, Dickens, and (most successfully) Robert Louis Stevenson turned some of their attention to children. Among our own country's established writers, Nathaniel Hawthorne wrote *A Wonder-Book* and *Tanglewood Tales*, and Mark Twain, *Tom Sawyer* and *Huckleberry Finn*. Writers who wrote almost exclusively for children were Louisa May Alcott, Frances Hodgson Burnett, Kate Douglas Wiggin, and Howard Pyle—to mention only a few. The monthly arrival of *St. Nicholas*, the children's magazine, was a stirring event in many thousands of households, and it was an honor for an author to be printed there.

Sadly enough, this wealth of well-written and imaginative literature was available only to children whose parents could afford to buy it. Poor children had to make do with what were known as "penny dreadfuls." While not as explicit as comparable material on the newsstands today, they covered the same ground—crime, violence, and sex. Not until 1900 were children allowed to withdraw books from public libraries.

And so, in a controlled but pleasantly free atmosphere, countless American middle-class childhoods passed under a serene blue sky. Nevertheless, there were clouds moving in as far as children's freedom was concerned, and the long Victorian children's picnic was nearly over. The turn of the century was a time of reform and moral uplift; while Ida Tarbell attacked the trusts and Lincoln Steffens was muckraking among the big city bosses, there were those who thought children needed an overhauling as well. As we will see in the following chapters, the concept of laissez-faire in child management went out. As a matter of fact, it went out so completely that when in the 1940s Dr. Spock brought it back in another form, people gave him the credit or blame for inventing it. *Plus ça change.* . . .

Birds and Bees
St. Nicholas, December, 1879

6
SACRED BUT NOT NICE

SOMETHING CALLED DELICACY OVERTOOK AMERICANS SOON after our successful Revolution. Like an incoming tide, it flowed all over the nineteenth century, reaching its high-water mark about a hundred years ago. From that point it slowly receded, leaving behind rock pools of what came to be identified as prudery. Today, with the tide at a record ebb, the word "delicacy" usually connotes either fragility or a choice food and certainly not "aversion to what is considered morally distasteful or injurious," which is what it chiefly meant to our ancestors.

The Puritans subscribed to moral strictness but not to delicacy in the nineteenth-century sense of the word. They called a spade a spade. A colonial lady or gentleman had no hesitation about using such words as "legs" and "belly" to describe those parts of the body; but their children and grandchildren preferred "nether limbs" and "lower portion." Perhaps one reason why this came about was that many families were rising into higher social spheres and felt insecure about how to behave there. They were, in fact, unwittingly fashioning the great American middle class, which was to become the arbiter and dictator of our manners and morals, replacing both church and monarchy. In colonial days most people had tried to behave in a blameless manner for fear of an avenging God. Fear of Mrs. Grundy had also been a factor, but now, in more worldly times, that lady assumed a little more importance and an outraged Deity a little less. As for the monarchy, which had been represented in the colonies by the royal governor and his circle, the citizens of the new Republic were eager to show that they despised it. Intensely patriotic, they were out to prove that the United States was the noblest, purest land on earth. Standards of propriety must therefore be lofty indeed, and the men relied on their wives to set these standards and to bring up the children in accordance with them. A squeamish female became the ideal, and girls grew up with the conviction that if they were properly squeamish, they would be thought refined.

One book that spelled out how delicacy could be achieved was *A Father's Legacy to His Daughters*, by John Gregory. Originally published in England, it was often reprinted in America during the late eighteenth and early nineteenth centuries. The clergyman author cautioned his readers not to be afraid of being thought prudish. "When a girl ceases to blush, she has lost the most powerful charm of beauty," he assured them. Young girls, he said, would be better off if they remained "rather silent" in company. "Wit is the most dangerous talent you can possess." As for humor, it is "often a great enemy to delicacy . . ." and so is learning ("if you happen to have any learning, keep it a profound secret, especially from the men . . ."). Apparently American girls took this advice to heart, for foreign visitors often complained of great difficulty in trying to engage them in ordinary conversation; and John Quincy Adams, as a young man around Boston, wished that "our young ladies were as distinguished for the beauties of their minds as they are for the charms of their persons. But alas! too many of them are like a beautiful apple that is insipid to the taste."

Considerations of delicacy also governed falling in love. ". . . Love is not to begin on your part" was the decree of Dr. Gregory. "[It] is entirely to be the consequence of our attachment to you. . . . As . . . nature has not given you that unlimited range in your choice which we enjoy, she has wisely and benevolently assigned to you a greater flexibility of taste on this subject. . . . If you love him, let me advise you never to discover to him the full extent of your love; no, not although you marry him; that sufficiently shows your preference, which is all he is entitled to know." Dr. Gregory further informs his audience that "violent love" (delicacy prevents him from clarifying this term) will lead to "satiety and disgust" and that it is a woman's job to avoid it.

To instill and foster delicacy in children became an increasingly vital element in their rearing. A child displaying indelicacy was sure to be barred from other children's houses by watchful parents. Table manners, dress, conversation, even the food one preferred involved questions of delicacy. A properly delicate girl, for instance, asked for a helping of white meat of chicken (never breast) and declined—at least in public—such robust items as corned beef or blood pudding. There were debates as to whether it was indelicate for girls to attend public lectures. Lydia Child, in 1833, defied majority opinion by writing that skating, hoop-rolling, and other boyish sports were suitable for little girls, but only "provided they can be pursued within the inclosure of a garden, or court; in the street, they would of course be highly improper. It is true, such games are rather violent, and sometimes noisy; but they tend to form a vigorous constitution; and girls who are habitually lady-like will never allow themselves to be rude and vulgar, even in play."

But the most crucial questions of delicacy revolved around "the natural functions" (excretion), "lying in" (childbirth), and that other activity for which not even a euphemism was possible. Old people left over from a coarser age were likely to distress their descendants by speaking of childbirth as if it were something that happened in a bed, not in heaven, or by guffawing and winking when the conversation turned to newlyweds. Bundling, that cozy custom of the colonials, was out. The very memory of it was shocking. In 1774, Philip Fithian, tutor in the Carter family, wrote in his diary that Fanny and Harriot, the two youngest girls, "by stuffing rags and other Lumber under their Gowns just below their Apron-Strings, were prodigiously charmed at their resemblance to Pregnant Women." It is quite likely that Fanny and Harriot's grandchildren did not even know what a pregnant woman was. From the 1790s on, every family strove to possess a parlor sofa, but even though it was narrow, upright, and covered in slippery horsehair, it could prove a trouble spot if one had teen-age daughters in the house. The European institution of the chaperon was scarcely known in this country until after the middle of the century. Young ladies were supposed to guard their own virtue. In the 1840s Dr. William Alcott, a cousin of Bronson Alcott, advised boys to watch for the slightest hint of "loose conduct" in girls and flee immediately if anything like it appeared.

Mrs. Lydia Sigourney, known as the Sweet Singer of Hartford, was full of advice for parents. She assured her readers that children are by nature delicate (in the moral sense) "unless contaminated by evil example. . . . Let this feeling be respected where it exists and implanted where it does not." And as an example of childish delicacy she told of a little boy who had chosen "of his own accord the most delicate manner of revealing a common pain" by announcing, "I am tired under my apron."

Mrs. Sigourney believed that children are born modest and "shrink from exposure of their persons." Perhaps that was the case in Hartford, but at about the same period in Cambridge, Mr. and Mrs. Nathaniel Hawthorne were giving their small boy and girl "air baths," which meant having them run about naked in a fire-heated room before bedtime. Since Mrs. Hawthorne was a rigid prude who edited her husband's work for words like "belly," we must surmise that she subscribed to a prevalent theory that children are entirely sexless, like cherubs, and if kept uncontaminated will remain so at least until puberty and, with luck, until they are married.

To pretend that sex did not exist seems to have been a common Victorian practice. Writing of his 1880s boyhood, the noted educator Henry Noble MacCracken recalls that on Sunday mornings the three MacCracken boys—aged about ten, twelve, and fifteen—and their eighteen-year-old sister all got into bed with their parents. He and his brothers snuggled close to Mamma, "who was warm and soft and comfortable all over," while their sister, a Bryn Mawr sophomore, was cuddled by Papa. And in this surprising tableau they all remained until time for church.

If children asked about sex, their indelicacy was attributed either to an evil influence—a servant or naughty playmate—or to "bad blood" (but, of course, that could hardly be the case with one's *own* children). The bad influence must be removed at once and the question responded to in a stern tone with "You are too young to understand" or "You must never talk about such things." In *Hints for the Nursery* (1863), Mrs. C. A. Hopkinson had an ingenious suggestion:

> A child early asks questions of his mother in relation to his own existence, which cannot be answered except by referring the subject in general terms to God. . . . It will be necessary for you to show him, using unintelligible terms, that you are quite right in saying he is too young to understand. . . . Say: "If you remember, the animal kingdom is divided into several parts. Of these parts, the mammalian do not, like the oviperous portion, perpetuate the race by the deposition of . . ." By this time, the little face shows great mystification.

"Kiss Me Quick"
Currier & Ives, Museum of the City of New York, Peters Collection

As the nineteenth century wore on, Americans devised ever more ways of being delicate. *The Bazar Book of Decorum* (1870) decreed that delicacy forbade the announcement of a birth in the newspaper, as was the custom in crass old Europe. Male friends of the new parents might call on the father but must not see the mother for four or five weeks. If possible, older children in the family should be sent for a visit with Grandma, returning to find that angels have brought them a tiny sister or brother. A baby shower would have been unthinkable—that is, before the birth—for when a woman was *enceinte* (it sounded more respectable in French), she did not speak of it, and neither did her friends.

Mother's Help and Child's Best Friend, by Carrica Le Favre (1890), suggested that one way of stamping out "lower instincts" in children was to forbid between-meal snacks; eating brings blood to the stomach, "thereby developing abnormally the lower instincts." Kite flying and a little club swinging before an open window would develop the higher instincts, which reside in the head and heart. On the other hand, marble playing would animalize children ("all back and no chest"). Kissing was sure to degrade both health and morals.

For parents of too-inquisitive youngsters a handy bit of scripture was "Know ye not that ye are the temples of the living God?" (and therefore ye must keep these temples pure, clean, and wholesome and not corrupt them with impure musings on the subject of sex). Nevertheless, toward the end of the century, there was a rising murmur of voices saying that if parents failed to impart a few concrete facts about sex, children would listen to pernicious and incorrect information. In the nineties a few timidly worded books and pamphlets appeared, most of them written by doctors or clergymen, that parents might obtain in a plain wrapper. They spoke lyrically of plants, oysters, and songbirds but seldom of higher forms of life, such as people. "Flowers," wrote Dr. Lyman Beecher Sperry (1893), "are but the reproductive organs of plants." And if these lovely things, which are picked by innocent little children and arranged in vases by irreproachably virtuous mothers, are reproductive organs, why "surely there is nothing inherently or necessarily indelicate or unclean" about sex. Mild as this news seems, it was not intended for children ("who have no practical use for information on these subjects"), but for young people old enough for courting. He warned girls against hand holding and kissing, because an honorable and cautious young man, though he might enjoy this sort of thing, will eventually "seek other young ladies for a better companionship. Be the sort of girl of whom it may be said, 'I know her; the worst thought she entertains / Is whiter than her pretty hand.' "

The most successful what-to-tell-them books were *What a Young Boy Ought to Know* and *What a Young Girl Ought to Know*, by Sylvanus Stall, a minister. They first appeared in the mid-nineties and were still being reprinted as late as 1936.

"If you have tried to deceive your child," says Stall, "it is probable that your child is now following your example and is trying to deceive you." If the child is forthright and puts the question "Where do babies come from?" Stall provides the parent with the following run-around:

> My dear child, the question you have asked is one that every man and woman, every intelligent boy or girl and even many very young children have asked themselves or others—whence and how they came to be in the world. If you were to ask where the locomotive and the steamship or the telegraph and the telephone came from, it would be wisest, in order that we might have the most satisfactory answer that we should go back to the beginning of these things, and consider what was done by George Stephenson and Robert Fulton, by Benjamin Franklin and Samuel Morse, by Graham Bell and Thomas Edison toward developing and perfecting these useful inventions.

Thus, Dr. Stall continues, to understand where babies come

from we must go back to Genesis and consider the mysterious manner in which God created Cain and Abel and their descendants. From Genesis, Stall suddenly changes the subject to cornstalks and their clever and attractive way of reproducing: the tassels are the fathers, and the newly forming ears are the mothers, and no hanky-panky. Stall then describes how Mamma and Papa Shad get little shad and then passes to birds, a subject on which he is more vague. "In the case of the birds, you may have noticed that there were two parent birds, the father bird and the mother bird." And after a while there are eggs, "which the mother produces in various ways." The high point of the story is reached when Stall reveals that in the case of mammals the egg is retained in the body "after being suitably fertilized."

After unloosing this blockbuster Stall turns to "Know ye not that ye are the temples of the living God?" and ends with a sermon.

Stall's bold pamphlets proved so successful that their author gave up the ministry and went into the publishing business. In a manual prepared for his force of door-to-door salesmen Stall told how to cope with every possible type of sales resistance. Apparently the most common objection of mothers was "I don't believe in telling children such things," to which the proper parry was a story of a girl of the streets who cried in anguish, "Ah, why did not my mother tell me?" Other objections were: "I've got a doctor book" (but not like this one, Ma'am); "I must ask my husband" (*you* are the one to impart information); "forty cents is too expensive" (it's worth its weight in gold); "children know too much already" (yes—too much misinformation); "I got along without such knowledge and my children can, too" (times have changed); "my child is too young" (but he will soon be older); and "the crops are a failure" (make a successful crop of your children).

Stall and his competitors in the sex-manual field dwelt at length on the horrors that must result from both masturbation and "sowing wild oats." There was nothing new, of course, in denouncing them. But in the late nineteenth and early twentieth centuries they had to be denounced in a whisper, whereas the colonials had denounced them in shouts from the pulpit or in the public press. Here, for example, is part of a front-page editorial in the Falmouth, Maine, *Gazette* for January 8, 1785, directed to adolescent boys:

> You have violent passions implanted in you by nature for the accomplishment of her purposes. But do not conclude, as many have done to their ruin, that because they are violent, they are irresistible. . . . Pray for divine assistance. Avoid solitude the first moment a loose thought insinuates itself and hasten to the company of those whom you respect. Never converse on subjects which lead to impure ideas. Have courage to decline reading immoral books, even when they fall into your hands. If you form a strong attachment to a virtuous woman, dare to marry early. It is better to be poor than wicked. . . . Thus shall you avoid the perpetual torment of unruly affections, the most loathsome of diseases, and the thousand penalties of selfish celibacy.

A generation later, delicacy forbade such frank language in a family newspaper; and by 1840, when Dr. William Alcott wrote a book called *A Young Man's Guide*, the young men who owned it were cautioned to keep it away from junior members of their families. Of "solitary licentiousness" Dr. Alcott said, "It is the lowest—I may say most destructive of practices," and went on to tell of a man in Pennsylvania whose wretched habits of this kind had rendered him, at thirty-five, tottering, wrinkled, and hoary. Alcott quoted Galen, Celsus, and Hippocrates, all of whom had agreed that "solitary vice" would bring feeble constitutions to generations yet unborn. The hospitals, he went on, were full of persons whom it had driven insane. Other consequences were Saint Vitus' Dance, epilepsy, palsy, blindness, apoplexy, hypochondria, consumption, and "a sensation of ants crawling from the head down along the spine. . . . And unless the abominable practice which produced all the mischief is abandoned, death follows."

Dr. Alcott's views on masturbation were all but universal at the time. A baby or small child who was observed to take an interest in its "parts" struck terror into the heart of its mother—especially if the baby was a girl, for this meant an unnatural sex appetite that would have to be ruthlessly curbed, perhaps by pills or even surgery. For Victorian young ladies a natural sex appetite was absolutely none at all. Sometimes, wrote Dr. Emma Drake in *What a Young Wife Ought to Know* (1901), a woman during pregnancy might be "troubled" with passion. "This . . . is due to some unnatural condition and should be considered a disease." Under normal conditions a wife will automatically preserve "the womanly modesty which characterized her girlhood," preferably in a separate bedroom, where it will be easier for her to avoid "a freedom which degenerates into license." As for the husband, conserving his seminal fluid "lifts him to a higher plane of being," and he ought to be grateful.

Apparently a good many children showed "evil propensities," for there were various restraining devices on the market, including tiny handcuffs and something called a thigh-spreader. Indeed, doctors often prescribed them. Children were warned that it was easy to tell secret self-abusers just by looking at them. One physician wrote, "When I see a little girl or young lady, wasted and weak, listless, with great hollow eyes and a sort of sallow tint on the haggard face, with the red hue of the lips faded, the ears white like marble and the face covered with pimples, I know that they have committed the sin which, if not abandoned will lead them down to death." A handbook for boys published in 1913 by the American Medical Association stated that some boys, instead of growing "into hard-muscled, fiery-eyed, resourceful young men," turned into "sissy young men and then into narrow-chested, flabby-muscled mollycoddles." This authoritative and prestigious book went on to say that "spermin" (a substance present in semen) is carried to the heart by the blood and then through the arteries "in a thrilling, throbbing stream" to the muscles. Also "this same wonderful substance" reaches the brain, where it contributes to clear reason and sound judgment, high ambitions and strong will. Masturbation (the word is not used) naturally interferes with all this.

Looking back from the 1970s we may well wonder how attitudes toward the unmentionable, from breasts of chicken on, could have changed so drastically. How did we arrive at our present unfettered state? Freud is widely held responsible, but in fact, although his teachings first reached this country in 1906, they had little effect in the average nursery until at least the 1930s. As far as child rearing is concerned, parents have always preferred the tried and true, and new theories take hold slowly. And certainly, for parents reared in Victorian days, it was easier to think of children as sexless cherubs than as victims of such alarming afflictions as Oedipus complexes and penis envy.

But long before Freud other forces for change were at work. Medical advances of the middle and late nineteenth century had produced a new interest in health and hygiene and therefore a more matter-of-fact attitude toward the human body. Exercise—in the form of either calisthenics or sports—came to be appreciated as healthy, and therefore wholesome, even for girls who might have to sacrifice some of their delicacy in the interests of good muscle tone. As early as the 1850s an English visitor, Lady Emmeline Wortley, was amazed to observe at a New England beach young females not only bouncing up and down in the gentle summer waves but sharing them with the opposite sex. Heterosexual public skating became decent only a few years later. "Health is coming into fashion," remarked the *Atlantic Monthly* for June, 1862. "A mercantile parent lately told me that already in his town if a girl could vault a five-barred gate, her prospects for a husband were considered to be improved ten per

Two innocent creatures
St. Nicholas, August, 1880

cent. . . ." When lawn tennis was invented in the seventies, girls insisted on being included even though it put them into an unladylike sweat ("glow," however, was the preferred term). In the nineties they bicycled; and at last—although not until about 1910—they achieved the major breakthrough of riding horseback astride.

Some responsibility for these developments surely rests upon Louisa May Alcott, whose books were standard fare for American girls from the late 1860s on. Her young heroines were robust and sensible—even, as in the case of Jo March, tomboyish. They came from country villages and gave themselves no airs. They coasted, ran, climbed, and romped with the boys, and they had robust and boyish appetites. In one Alcott story a group of girls consume a meal of corned beef and cabbage, baked beans and brown bread, beefsteak, potatoes, Indian pudding, and pumpkin pie "with appetites that would have destroyed their reputation as delicate young ladies if they had been seen."

Says Rose, the heroine of *Eight Cousins*, to her Uncle Alec, who is a doctor, "I'm too old for running, Uncle. . . . Miss Power said it was not ladylike for girls in their teens."

"I take the liberty of differing from Madame Prunes and Prisms and, as your physician, I order you to run. Off with you!" says Uncle Alec, adding that Rose ought to bathe in cold water each morning, throw away her tight belt, and learn to skate and swim with her boy cousins. *Eight Cousins* (1875) sets forth the ideal code of behavior for ordinary American middle-class adolescents of the period. In free and guileless camaraderie boys and girls went about in groups. They played games, pulled taffy, and even went on overnight hikes. Boys were expected to behave chivalrously and girls modestly; and they usually did so, for the penalty was ostracism. Flirting was frowned on, and a girl who permitted "liberties," such as hand holding, lost caste. Consequently a boy who wanted to hold hands or more—and there were no such boys in Miss Alcott's books—had to look for a partner in dance halls or amusement parks.

Wealthy parents could maintain a steady surveillance of their children with the help of nursemaids, governesses, and chaperons, but for most Americans this became increasingly difficult. With the rise of industrialization working-class children often had jobs that took them away from home for ten or twelve hours a day. Children who did not need to work went to public school, where they were thrown into daily contact with what the Puritans used to call "all sorts." And by 1900 it was a usual thing for girls to stay in high school until they graduated, along with the boys. Parents were warned to screen their children's friends. "Constant vigilance is the price parents must pay if they would keep their children pure," admonished one child-care book; and another, pointing out that any parent would be alarmed if his children were exposed to scarlet fever, asked, "Is there equal anxiety when a certain boy or girl in the community is thought to be a source of moral contamination?" Companions "of poor tone" must be driven away. "Run away, Henry Jones," Mother ought to say. "I won't have you play with my children in this yard."

Parents who imparted the story of cornstalks and shad were often dismayed to find their children ostracized as sources of contamination by other, less daring parents. But as time went on and the young ranged farther and farther from parental surveillance, there was increasing agitation in favor of some form of sex education. Not that it was called that. The gingerly term devised in the early 1900s was "social hygiene." The message that usually got through was that this is a sacred and solemn subject and your bodies are temples; but we aren't going to tell you much about it, and you must put it right out of your mind because it isn't nice. Says the author of *The Renewal of Life* (1906), "Very reverently explain that the mother cat has ovaries," but she stops short of even the most reverent discussion of tomcats. (The same author, however, dares to suggest that "desire is not abnormal in a girl.") Another advisor recommended that parental talks on sex should emphasize the pain of childbirth in order to "remove any tendency toward lascivious thought which the child might have otherwise." One little boy wept for hours when told of the agony he had caused his dear mamma in being born. The author of *Childhood* (1905) warned that information must be imparted "as delicately as possible." With girls "it seems to me a mistake to make unnecessary disclosures, which, however sacredly we may regard them, are more than apt to shock the sensibilities of the immature mind."

However delicately, sacredly, or frighteningly sex was presented to the young of the early 1900s, no method seems to have been a resounding success. And when that rising generation grew up and, in the 1930s, faced the problem of what to tell *their* children, they were nearly as perplexed as their parents had been. By that time a lot of taboos had been relaxed, and even the most delicate sensibilities had got used to short skirts, lipstick, one-piece bathing suits, the tango and the Charleston, and adolescents driving about by twos in automobiles. "None of our old ways prepare youth," commented one child-care writer. The experts were now advising parents to give children the facts and not confuse them with tales of the birds and bees. *Sex in Childhood* (1933) scolded parents for the "sacred but not nice" message. "Don't panic and shame the child for sexual offenses. Correct and divert him, in the same manner that you might say 'Keep out of that jar of raspberry jam, you rascal, you!' "

Few parents in the 1930s were able to equate sex with raspberry jam—which is hardly surprising. What *is* surprising is that today, after so many years of public discussion of sex and so much public exorcism of prudery, there still appear to be many parents who avoid the subject. Dr. Haim G. Ginott, in his best seller *Between Parent and Teenager* (1969), quotes a father who said,

"Sex may have gone as public as AT&T but I want no share in it." Masturbation still causes anxiety and concern despite at least fifty years of reassurance that it won't cause insanity or even pimples. The young still complain (again, according to Dr. Ginott), "I can't ask my mother anything about sex."

Can it be possible? Or is it that the tables are turned and it's the children, not the parents, who won't communicate? After all, what do Mom and Dad know compared to Dr. Reuben or Masters and Johnson or *Playboy*—all available at the corner drugstore for the price of a few ice-cream cones?

Those less fortunate than we
St. Nicholas, May, 1882

RICH CHILDREN,
POOR CHILDREN

SO FAR IN THIS BOOK WE HAVE BEEN TALKING ABOUT MIDDLE-
class children of Anglo-Saxon, Protestant background, whose
parents were able to feed, clothe, and educate them adequately if
not lavishly. Until the middle of the nineteenth century this
group of citizens was so numerous and so self-satisfied that when
they looked around they were under the impression that they
were the only Americans that mattered. They had little to do
with Americans of other than Anglo-Saxon origin—who, in
those years, were chiefly from northwestern Europe and Ireland.
Certain enclaves of these European groups retained their
language and culture and kept aloof from the American
mainstream. Others joined it, sometimes anglicizing their sur-
names. Those who did brought up their children in the
American manner and within a generation or two forgot their
other heritage. A rise in economic status usually produced this
result.

In colonial times, poverty in America was generally within bounds that the state could manage. Town or city authorities took care of orphans and of children of indigent parents by apprenticing them or binding them out as servants. The system of "vendering" was introduced about the time of the Revolution. This was a sort of public auction of dependent paupers—children, old people, cripples, and the insane. Citizens who needed help in their houses or on their farms, or who wanted a little extra cash, bid against each other for a weekly stipend to be paid by the town in return for offering lodging to a pauper. The lowest bidder took the pauper home with him. Thus there was a home of sorts available to every child, and sometimes even a good one. In the sprawling rural society that was northeast America then, very few families were really rich, but not many were in danger of starving.

But the Industrial age brought far greater extremes. By the second decade of the nineteenth century, the streets of the port cities were teeming with immigrants. Some of them found American life too much for them and became homeless and helpless. For these there were only the almshouses, where old and young, insane and terminally ill were mixed indiscriminately and vastly overcrowded. Municipal authorities were not ready for such unprecedented problems and if anything was done, private citizens did it. For example, in 1790 there were only three orphanages in the country: one in Boston, one in Philadelphia, and one in Georgia (there was another in not-yet-American New Orleans). Then, largely due to private initiative, in the space of a few years there were over fifty.

In New York City a group of civic-minded people established, in 1825, the House of Refuge for children who were either found wandering in the streets or who had been brought into court for minor crimes. The idea of helping the poor was still regarded by many as interfering with God's will, but a new concept, that of protecting society by taking potential criminals off the streets and reforming them early, found a receptive public and loosened purse strings that had previously been tightly closed to charity. The New York House of Refuge opened with a complement of sixteen boys and girls. The majority had done nothing illegal, but the daily routine was more like that of a prison than a home: ten hours of work, an hour and a half of study, no talking in the dormitories or dining hall, strict separation of the sexes, and almost no free time. Some of the children decided they preferred the streets and took French leave. The Board of Governors found the first superintendent too lenient and some of the later ones too severe. The children were exploited for their labor and the Ladies Auxiliary regularly lectured the girls in genteel, middle-class terms that meant little to them. But, despite its shortcomings, the House of Refuge was clearly a better place for a pauper child than the city almshouse or than sleeping under bridges and in alleys.

Other facilities for New York street children were established later, but they were never adequate. All through the nineteenth century, visitors to New York were horrified by the sad children they saw: tots of three or four, forced to dance to the music of an organ-grinder; child prostitutes; hungry, sick, freezing little faces on every hand. Charles Dickens, in the 1840s, found the Five Points area of Manhattan quite as distressing as the worst slums of London. And the heavy influx of immigrants after the Civil War produced even worse results.

Child labor in factories began decently enough in the early-nineteenth-century spinning mills of New England. The idea of children working in mills shocked almost no one, since children had always worked at home. Alexander Hamilton, speaking in the House in 1791, praised cotton mills for providing jobs for the unemployed. "It is worthy of particular remark," he said, "that in general women and children are rendered more useful, and the latter more early useful, by manufacturing establishments, than they would otherwise be."

The mills at Lowell, Massachusetts, worked their children hard, but kept a benign eye on their housing and welfare, so that the atmosphere was something like that of a strict boarding school. Many a farm girl worked there for several years in order to save enough money for a tiny dowry. But mill conditions elsewhere deteriorated as the century progressed. In Paterson, New Jersey, in 1835, six hundred children under sixteen worked for wages ranging from fifty cents to $1.75 a week. In summer the hours were from sunrise to sunset, with a half hour for breakfast and three-quarters of an hour for dinner. In winter the children worked from dawn to 8 p.m. with no time off for breakfast, which they had by candlelight before work began. Notwithstanding, if there was any public criticism of this state of affairs, it was to complain about cheap competition.

In the big cities, children began to work when they were no more than three—piecework like sorting feathers or leaves of tobacco. Many of them contracted respiratory diseases and died young; but since their living conditions were unsanitary and fraught with a hundred diseases, it was difficult to say that their work caused their death. The poor avoided the city hospitals, which had a reputation for being way stations en route to potter's field. As for the almshouses and foundling hospitals, their infant mortality rate was close to 100 percent. Mothers who abandoned ("dropped") their babies usually tried someone's doorstep rather than risk these terrible places.

The New York diarist Philip Hone, an elegant gentleman of the best society, was the recipient of a "drop" in 1842. He noted in his diary that the week-old boy was healthy and handsome and that the idea of keeping him crossed his mind. A locket containing a lock of hair was around its little neck, and there was a note to say that the mother was the penniless widow of a sailor drowned at sea. When the baby arrived, the Hones were entertaining friends at dinner. All the guests (one of whom was William Backhouse Astor) advised against keeping the waif. "It was one of the sweetest babies I ever saw," wrote Hone. But, "if the little urchin should turn out bad, he would prove a troublesome inmate; and if intelligent and good . . . the rightful owners might come and take him away." So he had the infant taken to the almshouse. It is interesting to note that no attempt was made to find and help the mother—which Hone, a former mayor of New York, might well have been able to do. The truth was that people in those days shrank from giving their name, legacies, or even protection to the child of unknown parents, for it was assumed that such people must have been weak or bad in some way or they would not be giving up their children. There were no adoption laws, probably because adoption was too rare to require legislation. The practice did not become common until well into the twentieth century. (England's first adoption law was enacted in 1926, and other countries have lagged even more.) In the nineteenth century, other solutions had to be found to the problem of homeless children, especially since the time-honored system of apprenticeship was dying out and most housewives preferred the cheap labor of Irish girls, who could be fired if not satisfactory, to the responsibility of keeping a bound child servant.

A New York philanthropist, Charles Loring Brace, found a practicable answer and rescued thousands of boys and girls from the city streets. In 1854 he founded the Childrens Aid Society, whose greatest work was sending trainloads of indigent children west to the frontier states and territories, where they were taken into the homes of farmers. The system was called "placing out," and although sometimes the families did not like the children or vice versa, by and large placing out seems to have worked remarkably well. Brace was adept at collecting funds from wealthy city people on the grounds that to support the Childrens Aid Society was to rescue the cities from hordes of future criminals. The Society also maintained hostels for New York newsboys, where, for a few pennies, they found food and shelter.

Brace, as a child, had been a parishioner of Horace Bushnell, the author of *Christian Nurture* (see Chapter 5) and subscribed to the Bushnell theory that a child is a tabula rasa, a white sheet of paper on which life may write well or badly. General public opinion veered in this direction for perhaps a generation, but then tended to prefer social Darwinism, which taught that juvenile delinquents are a throwback to the savage past of the race and therefore cannot be reformed. Even Brace, in later life, believed in "gemmules," which were supposed to be latent tendencies working in the blood and giving good or bad stimuli to the brain and nerves. He felt, however, that if bad gemmules were treated early with kindness, firmness, and plenty of religion, delinquent children could be saved for civilization.

Social scientists of the nineties and early 1900s took the idea of gemmules even further. Many of them agreed with the psychologist G. Stanley Hall that all childhood is a savage time, "when the very worst and best impulses in the human soul struggle against each other for its possession," and that adolescence is naturally full of storm and stress and even criminality, of which street gangs are a normal part. Hall and his colleagues tried to prove their theories through physical measurement of delinquent children, and came up with some rather bizarre conclusions—such as that long-headed children are worse than others, and that bright boys are more sensitive to heat. One of Hall's students, Arthur Macdonald, operating on funds provided by the Bureau of Education, said that delinquent children have a "certain animality in the face," a low forehead, large jaw, and prominent ears—in short, they resemble cavemen and, furthermore, they won't look you in the eye. Another investigator, Thomas Travis, came to the same conclusions and carried them a step further: he suggested that delinquency might be cured by surgery to change the shape of the skull. Failing that, "for those who are not amenable to reformation there is only one realm left, and that is extirpation."

Authorities at reform schools and prisons stopped short of extirpation, but some of them went as far as castration and sterilization. In 1905, several hundred boys at the Indiana state reformatory were sterilized. The Commissioner of the New York State Board of Charities recommended "permanent sequestration" and "asexualization" of hopeless types. He spoke of the "filthy stream" of immigrants from southern Europe that "mingles itself with the purer waters of our communities." There were a number of attempts to lock up delinquent girls until they were too old for childbearing—"to prevent the transmission of moral insanity," as one social scientist (a woman) put it. Before 1946, there were 45,127 sterilizations performed legally in thirty states, and an unknown but probably not inconsiderable number illegally.

The story of poor and delinquent children does not have a happy ending. As we all know and read in the newspapers every day, our big cities still have overcrowded jails, where young first offenders are thrown in with hardened criminals; reform schools still have a large percentage of recidivists; and there are still homeless and suffering children. The greatest improvements we can point to are that in most states illegitimacy is not the stigma it once was; and healthy infants without homes are sure to be adopted—if they are white (but if they are nonwhite, handicapped, or older than a few months, they will probably spend their childhoods in foster homes).

As poor children grew more wretched during the nineteenth century, rich children became increasingly coddled and privileged. During the early 1800s, there were no Midas-rich citizens, and the upper classes were distinguished from other people more by manners than by possessions. The "first circle" of every city was a small, close-knit group with a few distinguishing caste marks: Their houses were big enough to accommodate dinner parties and balls; they kept a carriage and coachman; if they lived in the city (and most of them did, for their wealth usually derived from trade), they lived in the "right" section of town; they attended a certain "right" church; they subscribed to concerts and lectures, and, in New York, to the opera; and they went away in summer, either to their own country houses or to one of the resorts. But even lacking money for some of these things, they were still acceptable to other members of the first circle if they had good manners and belonged to an old family—that is, one that had been in Society for at least a couple of generations. According to Mrs. John King Van Rensselaer, a grande dame of New York, "one never thought whether this or that family had money or not."

Children of these certain families found their friends only among children of their parents' friends and rarely knew anyone well outside their circle, unless from a similar circle in another city. They were privately tutored or attended classes in which a small number of their peers were taught together. Their parents did not send them to public school if any other mode of education was available; if unavailable, the privileged children formed a coterie in the public school, a sort of junior "first circle," ignoring the others. Harriet Martineau, visiting America in the 1840s, was disconcerted at finding so much snobbery among children of the great American democracy. One little girl told her that formerly there had been no "sets" at her school, but that several grocers' daughters had enrolled and it was now necessary for the "higher" girls to form sets and to refuse to admit outsiders. Miss Martineau found solace in remembering that the so-called aristocracy of America was not large enough to be dangerous. "It cannot choose its own members, restrict its own members, or keep its gentility from contamination."

She was a perceptive lady. N. P. Willis, the New York journalist and wit of the same period, described the American elite as "flying-fish aristocracy," pointing out that not more than two thousand families in the whole country had been rich for two

Charity
Our Young Folks, 1865

or more generations and that the children of three-fourths of these would probably have to work for a living. A flying-fish aristocracy was especially observable in New York. At the beginning of the century, the leading families were descendants of Dutch and English colonial aristocrats. Fifty or seventy-five years later, the new flying fish were the Astors and the Vanderbilts and dozens of highly successful men who had risen from the humblest of backgrounds.

Despite the dire warnings of every child-care advisor from John Locke on, families who could afford plenty of servants were likely to entrust their children to them a good part of the time. Fashionable mothers hired wet nurses if they could find them, and established a separate nursery world on the top floors of their houses—despite the fact that the temperature close to the roof was likely to be too hot in summer and too cold in winter. Children were not omnipresent in wealthy households, as they were in middle-class ones. Philip Hone, whose diary reveals the manners of the New York upper classes in the 1840s, seldom mentions children at all, except to record their births or deaths.

The boy children of rich city families played in the street, but not with street children. Henry Cabot Lodge, for example, who grew up in Boston in the fifties, played on the Common, but his companions were Cabots and Lowells. If they did play with humbler children, they were careful not to bring them home. Small brothers and sisters were taken for walks by nursemaids or to a locked park where they met only their social equals. In New York, in the thirties and forties, they went to St. John's Park, which, together with its beautiful residential square, disappeared in toto when the railroad was laid down Ninth Avenue. Later, the exclusive place for hoop-rolling was Gramercy Park.

When the little girls were old enough for school, they were taught, besides the three Rs, a smattering of French and German, as well as embroidery, chirography, and music. Boys were educated separately from their sisters, and generally speaking, if they showed talent for the business world they were not expected to prepare for college. A German nobleman, Baron Grund, who visited Boston during the 1830s, was startled to hear a wealthy parent say, "I have brought up my sons to become merchants and manufacturers; only Sam, the poor boy who is a little hard of hearing and rather slow of comprehension, shall go to college." Of course, this was not the thinking of old Brahmin families, who prized a classical education, but there were a number of men in Boston who had risen to power without much education and therefore saw no need for it. One of them told the Baron, "I give my daughter to any man who will come to Boston and have wit enough to make a hundred thousand dollars in six years."

After transatlantic steamships began making regularly scheduled runs, the American rich began to go abroad in numbers, taking their children to acquire a little polish. European customs, particularly English ones, were among the souvenirs they brought back. Old-fashioned people like Philip Hone (who himself had risen from the ranks, his father having been a joiner), deplored the Europeanization of New York, and the importation of the chaperone. N. P. Willis wrote, in 1855, that among the "considerable and innocent privileges of the restrained sex" had been to go to the theatre with a gentleman, and to ride alone on an omnibus—but that these little pleasures were now to be forbidden. This state of affairs had long existed in England—Jane Austen, for example, could not travel alone to London in the stagecoach and was in her twenties before she ventured upon a solitary walk in the country. New York was the most ready convert to imported customs. Henry James's Daisy Miller, it will be remembered, while visiting Rome, committed the faux pas of going to the Colosseum unchaperoned and at night, too—but she was from the Middle West.

Girls (well-chaperoned) and boys attended dancing school together, one evening a week, but otherwise saw little of each other until it was time for the girls to make their debuts, which they did at seventeen. ("Coming out" was another imported custom, not usual in American society until midcentury.) A girl was considered a child until then, and her life was quiet, well-regulated, and uneventful. One proper New York child of the thirties and forties remembered Fourth of July as a highlight of each year because on that day her father took all his children to City Hall Park to watch the military companies on parade. Another thrill was to cross the Hudson to Hoboken on a Sunday afternoon and walk with Father along the wooded shore.

Society (with a capital S) changed very much after the Civil War. First, there were a number of people who had made money during the war and were anxious to join the elite. The old guard called them "Shoddy" or "The Shoddies" and refused to have anything to do with them. The successful newcomers had enormous fortunes—Rockefeller, Carnegie, Vanderbilt, Gould, and many others. These people expected a great deal of their children, who were to carry on dynasties. Many of them were brought up in the style of European nobility, with French or German governesses and English nannies rather than the simple Irish-immigrant nursemaids of the previous generation.

Mrs. William K. Vanderbilt was probably the first (but not the last) American mother to raise her daughter to wear a coronet. Young Consuelo Vanderbilt sat with a steel rod down her spine while she did her many hours of arduous lessons. When she misbehaved, which was seldom, her mother personally administered a punishment by whipping her on the legs with a riding crop. Ordinarily, she and her brother saw their parents only for an hour a day—after nursery supper—and even this visit consisted, as a rule, in sitting silently and listening to grown-up conversation. After Consuelo had learned to speak French, she was required to address her parents in that language only. At Newport, when she was in her early teens, she was never permitted to play tennis or any other sport with boys, as other girls did. At seventeen, the same year she came out, she married, unwillingly, the Duke of Marlborough.

An etiquette book of 1887, by "Anon," lays down a daily program for families of substance. The children are to take their breakfast with their governess an hour earlier than their parents. The governess has complete power, even when the mother is present, and she will seize this opportunity to correct table manners. She will then walk to school with the elder girls. After breakfast, Father asks to see the small children—"their coming to say good morning and goodbye is a delight when children are carefully reared." Mother now spends an hour or more in the nursery, and sees all the children again at luncheon. If there are no guests they will eat with her in the dining room. "An intimate and trusted friend of the family whose conversation will not lower the tone of the child's ideals, or the mother's standards, is now and then admitted to this mid-day meal."

The children's afternoon is spent in walking, driving, attending dancing school, and so on. All under the age of thirteen eat supper at six in the nursery. The older ones will dine with their parents, provided there are no guests. A girl who is not "out" is not considered "sufficiently intelligent to be interesting to her elders among her own sex, and certainly not worldly-wise enough to associate with gentlemen. . . ." In "best society she is never seen at a party that is composed of mature people outside of her father's house, previous to the finishing of her education." No instructions are given for teen-age boys, but presumably they are not fit for society either. As for the younger children, they are never to visit the drawing room except for birthdays or weddings, and even then if they are "over-hilarious" out they go. At Sunday lunch, they get to eat with Father—"and there is a general endeavor to make him feel that he is an honored guest at their dinner." Each child has a birthday party each year, with games, a simple meal, and no presents.

Apparently, Anon's book was not read in Chicago, or at

least not by the Marshall Field family. They gave a "Mikado" party for their children, and set up an entire stage set from a Gilbert & Sullivan company in the front hall of their mansion. There were expensive Japanese favors and a full dance orchestra. Young Marshall, aged seventeen, invited two hundred friends, and his sister Ethel, aged twelve, another two hundred.

It was certainly true that etiquette rules varied from city to city. In Boston, for instance, a group of debutantes might go to a party together with "a hack driver of the highest respectability." But in New York there was no hack driver respectable enough to take the place of a chaperone. "It seems hardly necessary to say," wrote the author of *Social Customs* (1887), "that a young lady must never go to a restaurant with a young man unless a chaperone accompanies them; neither must she go on an excursion of any sort. Especially should she avoid the fascinations and uncertainties of a sailboat. . . . If the boat be becalmed . . . a sailing-party is sometimes obliged to stay out all night." As late as 1922, when Emily Post wrote her first *Etiquette*, sailboats were still regarded as moral traps.

Even though the proper upper-class teen-ager was supposed to be stifled, this was often not the case. In earlier America, mothers took a back seat and attention was focused on daughters. Henry James called it "the social suppression of parents"—an American phenomenon, quite different from Europe. Very young ladies, some perhaps not more than thirteen, had better and more elaborate clothes than their mothers, and even received callers and presided at the dinner table. It all gave Henry James an idea for a story, mentioned in his notebooks— "the shunted mother—idea of the mother consenting temporarily to be *dead* (as it were) to help the daughter *through* something— some social squeeze. . . ." He eventually wrote a story on this theme, "Fordham Castle."

After World War I, the old rules governing the behavior of young people in Society began to collapse. Mrs. Van Rensselaer, a very old lady when she wrote *The Social Ladder* in 1924, complained that there was no more decorum, no more cotillion orchestras, and that any young persons could get in to a party if they had been to the right boarding school, could smoke and drink, and were "schooled to the astonishing intimacies of the present-day dances and the amazing candor of current Society conversation. . . ." Mrs. Post, in a 1929 edition of *Etiquette*, omitted all mention of sailboats.

New England gravestone: a child named Peter Bancroft
Photograph by Allan Ludwig
Index of American Design, National Gallery of Art

8

GLEETS AND HUMORS

Death is a Fisher-man, the World We see
His fishpond is, and we the Fishes Be. . . .
(children's verse, 1705)

ONE BEAUTIFUL APRIL MORNING IN 1721, COTTON MATHER
preached a sermon he had written especially for children. He
told them that more than half of them would be dead before the
age of seventeen. ("Children, it is your dawning time. It may be
your dying time. . . .") Unfortunately, he was right. The
eighteenth century was to bring many changes for the better, but
not in this respect. And when the confident, ambitious young
United States began the nineteenth century, it was with very
little more knowledge about the physical care of its children than
the first colonists had brought over from the Old World.

The field of medical care for children was a sparsely planted
one. There was not even a word for it; "pediatrics" was not
coined until the 1880s. In fact, in 1800 there was not one
physician in America who had made a special study of it and the
few books on the subject were by Englishmen or Europeans. In *A
Treatise of the Acute Diseases of Children* (1742), the author, Dr.

Walter Harris, noted, "I know very well in how unbeaten and almost unknown a Path I am treading."

The greatest destroyers of the young, especially of infants, were diseases of the digestive tract, known as the bloody flux, the watery gripes, the summer sickness, and cholera infantum. Next came the common childhood diseases—measles, mumps, whooping cough, scarlet fever, and diphtheria. Some parents, noting that these illnesses were more likely to be fatal in later life than in earlier, grimly sent their children into houses or schools where they might become infected. Tuberculosis and other lung diseases were the third great scourge; and, in the South, "the burning ague," or malaria. Appendicitis was "an iliac passion." Smallpox, once at the top of the list, was, by 1800, held in check by vaccination.

Children who escaped disease were not infrequently burned or scalded at busy kitchen fireplaces; or they set fire to their clothes with candles; or they tumbled into wells or brooks or under the hooves of horses. The minor scratches and cuts that children always experience could prove fatal if infection set in. And, probably more often than anyone realized, children died of whatever cure was being tried out on them. Pharmacies were not restricted from selling potent drugs to anyone, no questions asked; and parents, guided by one of the medical treatises imported from England, undertook to mix for their infants the most staggering combinations of dangerous drugs—antimony, mercury, opium, and "the bark" (quinine) being particular favorites. Home remedies were less dangerous, but apt to be ineffective; for diarrhea, powdered chalk in gruel; to cure whooping cough, "frighten the child"; for stomachaches, burned brandy, water, and sugar, every hour; for earache, a hot roasted onion (applied to the ear, not eaten); for "gleets and humors," ants' eggs and onion juice; for the common baby's ailment called thrush, a live frog, tied in a muslin bag and suspended around the patient's neck; for bad dreams, powdered peony seeds.

Harris's *Treatise* stated that the cause of infant diseases was acidity and that the cure, therefore, should be alkali—things like powdered crabs' claws or mashed pearls. Worms were a common complaint among children. "These worms are very small," wrote one English physician, "and are bred in the Skin, and the Heads of them appear like black hairs upon Friction in a Bath; they are generated by vitious Matter shut up in the Capillary Veins, turned into Worms when transpiration is hindered." Pewter filings in treacle was suggested to remove the worms (if it did not remove the child).

Teething pains, when a necklace of deer's teeth failed to help, were ministered to by lancing the gums or applying leeches to them. In fact, there was hardly any ailment not treatable by leeches. One of the most usual sights in a colonial sickroom—as familiar as a thermometer is today—was a small wooden box wherein the leeches resided in moist clay.

The first American physician to write about the physical care and illnesses of children was William P. Dewees, who practiced medicine in Philadelphia. His book, *A Treatise on the Physical and Medical Treatment of Children*, was first published in 1825 and was reprinted many times for half a century. "This subject, though deserving of consideration, is almost new in this country," he began. Some of his ideas seem elementary today but were then much in advance of the time. He reduced the extremely high mortality rate of bottle-fed babies by such innovations as keeping the bottles very clean, bringing the milk to the boil and then cooling it rapidly (as in pasteurization), and of making a formula of one-third cow's milk, one-third water, and sugar. Glass bottles were introduced about 1800, but rubber nipples not until 1835. Dewees suggested that a heifer's teat be fitted over the bottletop—it was easier to keep clean than a sponge or old rag.

Another very modern suggestion of Dewees was that Father might help with the baby—even as Cato, Augustus, Henry IV of

France, and Montaigne are said to have done. But, he added resignedly, Father would probably feel disgraced if he did so. Dewees attacked various old wives' tales, such as that flannel, unlike any other fabric, need not be washed or cleaned, and that wet diapers toughen the child by means of the salt in the urine (as salt toughens a herring). Diapers should always be clean and dry and must be secured with ties—never with buttons (which the wearer might consider edible) or straight pins, and certainly not with needles. He recounted a fearful tale of a baby who was wasting away from a tumor on its hip—until it was discovered that the tumor was caused by a needle, used months before to fasten a diaper and embedded in the poor child's flesh. (Fortunately for infants—and their mothers—the safety pin was about to be invented.)

Another writer on medical care for children was Dr. William Alcott, cousin of Bronson Alcott, whose *The Young Mother* first appeared in 1836. He quoted Dewees often and added observations of his own, drawn from long experience as a Massachusetts country doctor. Like Dewees and almost everyone in that day, Dr. Alcott believed in prenatal influence, as well as in the theory that moral characteristics can be imbibed with breast milk. He agreed with Dewees that the good conduct of the mother, not only during pregnancy but for years before, bore a direct relation to the character of her children. Nothing is said about the conduct of the father.

Dr. Alcott scolded mothers who shirked breast-feeding. Good wet nurses were hard to find and "even admitting what is claimed by some, that the temper of the nurse does *not* affect the properties of the milk and thus injure the child both physically and morally, still much injury may and inevitably will result from the influence of her constant presence and example— . . . her principles, manners and habits may *so* differ from the parents'. . . ." Bottle-feeding was to be considered a last resort; nor would a bottle baby's slim chances for survival improve if the mother or nurse followed the ancient practice of pre-chewing food for him, or of letting him suck on her lip.

Cold baths? "I am aware, that in rejecting the cold bathing of infants, I am treading on ground which is rather unpopular, even with medical men." At least, Alcott advised, wait until the child is six months old and then get him accustomed to cold water gradually; and *don't* (apparently some people did) put him to bed wet!

The advice of Dewees and Alcott was soon widely plagiarized, for American parents were pathetically eager for books on child care. Nearly all the new experts complained of the way the young were usually dressed. Although children were no longer encumbered with scaled-down copies of adult clothing, and little girls no longer had to wear busks (straight pieces of bone, to keep their backs straight), there still were problems. Babies were often hampered by long, heavy dresses and tight caps. Little boys wore stiff stocks and thick cravats, which Alcott said pressed on the jugular vein and hindered muscular development. "What can be more painful than to see little boys . . . walk as if they were fettered and trussed up for the spit; unable to look down or turn their heads . . . and only capable of using their arms to dangle a cane, or carry an umbrella, as they hobble along, perhaps on a hot sun-shiny day in July or August?" As for little girls, their clothing was likely not to be warm enough; and on a cold day they could not even run or walk at a fast clip because that was considered unladylike. "What can be a more pitiable sight than one of our modern girls going home from school or church in winter? Thinly clad, her skin has a leaden hue; her teeth chatter; her very heart is chilled in her panting, frozen bosom; she cannot run, and if she could she must not, for it would be vulgar!"

The old-fashioned way with babies was to keep them hot and swathed. The new books urged a nursery temperature of 65 to 70 degrees, frequently aired. And it was better to leave the floor bare, even though toddlers might take harder falls on it, because of the difficulty of keeping a carpet really clean. It is unfortunate, said Dr. Alcott, that many people smear earth on the skin as a cure-all, cherishing the erroneous belief that "dirt is healthy," because farm children are often healthier than the children of the rich.

So far, so good. The leading authorities agreed that the young need mothers' milk, fresh air, loose clothing, and cleanliness. Other matters were more controversial: for example, there were still voices raised against vaccination. Even much later, in 1890, one writer on child care (not a doctor, of course) voiced the formerly widespread conviction that vaccination was "morally perilous." She wrote, "It is irrational to say that any corrupt matter taken from boils and blisters of an organic creature could affect the human body otherwise than to injure it."

There was constant disagreement as to whether a baby should be rocked in a cradle, jumped, trotted, or in any way joggled about with the idea of amusing him. James Underwood, an eighteenth-century English authority widely read in America, said that cradles were good for children because they reminded them of prenatal days; but that they should not be furiously "jumbled about like travellers in a mailcoach." Another Englishman, William Cadogan, was of the opinion that babies ought to be "tumbled and toss'd about a good deal." Dr. Alcott was against tossing, especially after meals.

The controversy raged on through the century. Mrs. Tuthill (1855) thought something might be said for cradles, but tossing would derange the nervous system. Mary Ellen Chase, the novelist, recalls in her memoirs of an 1880s and 1890s childhood, spending two or three hours every afternoon rocking her baby brother's cradle. Dr. Seguin (1871) thought cradles should be built in the shape of the womb. May Blake (1883) anticipated modern theories with the comment that everything depends on the individual baby—some might thrive on rocking and tossing, while others might loathe it.

And where should young infants sleep? Despite the frequency with which infants were "overlain" and smothered by sleeping adults, many advisors thought the mother or nurse should hold the baby most of the day and sleep with it in her arms at night. Dr. Alcott disagreed, citing the case of a young mother whose infant slipped from her grasp while she slept, fell to the floor, and fatally fractured its skull. Mrs. Tuthill told with indignation of an old nurse who in July slept with a baby in a curtained bed heated with a warming-pan, and force-fed it with thick, hot pap ("to prevent wind from getting into its stomach"). As this child, not surprisingly, was "sickly and fitty," the nurse was also plying it with beer, spiced wine, and patented opiates.

Perhaps the most vexing problem of all was whether a baby should be picked up when he cries or left screaming. Alcott's view was that a certain amount of crying promotes circulation and strengthens the lungs, but he regretted that "we sometimes hear about children's crying themselves to sleep, as if it were a matter of no consequence; and sometimes as if it were, on the contrary, rather desirable." Mrs. Tuthill said she could see nothing salutary in violent crying spells, and added firmly that if an infant were fretful there must be something wrong with the mother or nurse. "Infants," she said, ". . . are naturally inclined to cheerfulness." Mrs. Hopkinson (1863) said flatly, "Babies should not be allowed to cry" and should be picked up and soothed before they get going. "The moment he begins his crying, let all your efforts be directed to stop it." And, furthermore, if he develops a bad temper it will be your fault. "It is well we cannot see all the consequences of our misdoings and shortcomings in education, or we should dread being parents." (Intimations of twentieth-century psychiatry.)

As for food, Dr. Alcott was a good deal ahead of his contemporaries in vehemently denouncing sweets—although not for the reason that they are bad for the teeth. Besides spoiling the appetite and overworking the stomach, he believed them intellectually overexciting and morally deleterious. Not only might a child meet bad company at a candy shop and go "from these places of pollution directly to the grogshop, the gambling house or the brothel," but he also would become dissatisfied with plain food and therefore with plain living, "the society of friends and the quiet discharge of our duty to God and our neighbor. . . . The young of both sexes who are in the use of confectionary are on the high road to gluttony, drunkenness, or debauchery; perhaps to all three." Some may have felt that Dr. Alcott was somewhat overstating his case. But when he added that commercial candy could be lethal, he was on firm ground; the colorings used were often poisonous enough to kill a child.

A plain, light diet for children had been urged by every expert since Locke. Judging by the insistence with which they kept urging it, many children must have been nourished chiefly on mince pie, pickles, salt pork, and various alcoholic potions. Mrs. Trippe (1881) recommended strengthening one's children by feeding them wine whey—milk and sherry simmered fifteen minutes, skimmed, and more sherry added. Dr. Thrailkill (1869) reported his amazement at finding the mouth of an hour-old infant crammed with "a huge slab of old, fat, raw bacon." It had been put there on the advice of the baby's grandmother. A little later, the child was treated to a brandy toddy, laced with soothing drops. Dr. Thrailkill believed that unsuitable food, liquor, and drugs accounted for at least 65 percent of infant deaths. In this he was undoubtedly right. More questionable was his further assertion that most of the other 45 percent died of bad heredity—that is, because the parents were too young, too far apart in age, or too closely related, or because of "the state of the parents at the time of conception and incompatibility of temperament, as two lymphatics." A lymphatic temperament was one of the categories into which the human race was divided by phrenologists, the others being sanguine, bilious, melancholic, nervous, choleric, and phlegmatic. Parents often took their children to phrenologists, who analyzed their temperaments according to the bumps on their skulls. Although not much hope was held out for a basically bad temperament, special diet and management might mitigate it and develop the "higher powers."

A child of "choleric" temperament might be calmed down by a light diet—but "light" had a different meaning in those days when the normal daily fare was considerably more abundant than it is now. An average middle-class child of the nineteenth century might sit down at breakfast to creamed eggs and dried beef, baked potatoes, pancakes, and cornbread. Dinner (the midday meal) was likely to be a meat pie, with several fried or creamed vegetables, bread, and a pudding with brandy sauce. The final meal of the day, known as tea, was lighter than the first two, but nearly always included some form of cake, pudding, or hot bread, accompanied by stewed fruit and cream. There were always bread, pastry, potatoes, and creamed dishes on the table and nobody knew about calories. Common-sensical Dr. Alcott pointed out that there was probably a connection between the skin eruptions that many young people suffered from and the large amounts of pastry they consumed. He recommended pure water rather than tea, coffee, or alcohol; raw rather than cooked fruit; and a minimum of salt. He added, "bread containing wood and bark affords little nutriment." Modern nutritionists would agree with him, but might wonder at his opinion of salads and herbs: "In the midst of such an abundance of excellent food as this country affords, it is most surprising that anybody should ever take it into their heads to eat such crude substances." As for nuts, they "are probably made for other animals rather than man."

Whether because American young people ate too much pie or did not exercise enough or studied too hard or did not air their rooms, many of them seem to have suffered ill health. Foreign visitors were apt to remark that American youth seemed subject to pale, sallow, waxen complexions. When the girls were pretty

Sickbed scene
St. Nicholas, December, 1879

they were very pretty—"the prettiest on earth," according to the British minister to Washington during the first Jefferson administration. But they were likely to be languid and to fade early. Why? Americans themselves blamed the climate, with its extremes of heat and cold. Dr. Combe, the English phrenologist, who toured the country in 1841, said rather bluntly that American females needed more baths. "Almost every house in Philadelphia built within fifteen years has a bath, but ladies either don't use them or don't remain long enough to enjoy the full benefits." An English visitor of 1819 pointed out that consumption carried off many young girls, "and may be generally traced to some foolish frolic, such as returning from a ball in an open sleigh or walking upon snow in their slippers." Others commented more sharply that American girls were simply spoiled and lazy. Their mothers failed to teach them housekeeping and they led a "harem life," lounging about in rocking chairs in darkened rooms. The Honorable Amelia M. Murray, who made an extensive tour in 1856, called American girls dolls, self-indulgent Asians, who devoted an hour to performing toilettes that an English girl would finish in ten minutes. She theorized that "the excitements and anxieties of business life probably entail constitutional delicacy upon the children of parents so eagerly occupied." Above all, the Honorable Amelia and her fellow Britons blamed lack of exercise. A Mrs. Baxter, whose visit took place in 1855, remarked, "As to roaming in the woods or climbing hills, they would regard anyone who proposed such a thing as a madman."

One trouble was that exercise was generally considered boyish and therefore improper for genteel young females. "Ought female children to receive the same education as boys and have the same scope for play?" inquired *The Catechism of Health* (1815); and it answered itself, "In their earlier years there should be no difference. But there are shades of discretion and regards to propriety which judicious and prudent guardians and teachers can discern and can adjust and apply." Said Mrs. Tuthill, who was given to high-flown language, "The softness in the man ought to be latent, and should only issue at some heavenly call. The courage in a woman should sleep, as the light sleeps in the pearl." (This was a strictly nineteenth-century concept; in colonial days a man might weep in public and a woman was expected to show plenty of no-nonsense courage.) Catherine Sedgwick, in a book of advice for girls, knew she was risking severe criticism when she advised her readers to get an education and be capable of independence. "They will say that to talk about developing a woman's reason and claiming her natural rights is very unfeminine . . . [they] will talk to you of the gentle sway of beauty, of the charm of sensibility, the loveliness of female dependence. . . . Women as yet, for the most part, have exercised but half their powers." Still, Miss Sedgwick added hastily, women should not try to vote or to enter the professions. "Training a son is the greatest work."

Another hindrance to young people running about and exercising was the old Puritan prohibition against frivolity of any kind, even including laughter. Dr. Alcott urged his readers to remember that laughter, like crying, exercises the lungs. Many people, he said, believed that Jesus never laughed. "The common notion in this subject, if not ridiculous, is certainly strange. . . . I have seen many parents who were miserable because their children were sporting and joyful." Children of such parents were apt to form the habit of putting their hands over their mouths to conceal laughter. "Mama, I see part of your smile," said little Una Hawthorne, observing her mother with one hand over her mouth. An upstate New York woman who grew up in the 1850s remembered that her grandmother never laughed or smiled; when something amused her, she would cover her mouth and go quickly out of the room.

Dr. Alcott went on to complain, "All our family arrangements tend to repress amusement. Everything is contrived to facilitate business; especially the business or employments of adults. The child is hardly regarded as a human being. . . . There may indeed be here and there a child's chair, or a child's carriage, or newspaper, or book; but there will seldom be, except by stealth, any free juvenile conversation at the table or the fireside. Here the child must sit as a blank or a cypher, to ruminate on the past, or to receive half-formed and passive impressions from the present."

Alcott was certainly describing a typical Calvinist household, of which he must have seen many as he made his doctor rounds in villages of western Massachusetts. It seems curious that none of the stifled children he described came to the attention of foreign visitors, who consistently found American children spoiled, pert, impudent, "forward without genius, talkative without information," and generally intolerable. Possibly they never saw rural children from conservative homes, but only children in cities or in hotels or traveling in public conveyances.

Anthony Trollope, traveling through America in 1862, remarked upon a lack of rosy cheeks in American children and attributed it to hot, stuffy houses and too many beefsteaks and pickles. "They eat and drink just as they please; they are never punished; they are never banished, snubbed, and kept in the background . . . and yet they are wretched and uncomfortable." Trollope was observing families who lived in hotels and boarding houses, as many did for months or even years at a time. Harriet Martineau thought boarding-house children rather pathetic. "It is melancholy to see girls of twelve years old either slinking down beside their parents and blushing painfully as often as any one of fifty strangers looks toward them; or boldly staring at all that is going on, and serving themselves like little women of the world." She, too, noticed their lack of good health.

Mary Duncan, another English traveler of the fifties, was kinder—or, at any rate, more polite—than the rest. She thought one might at first call American children impudent but on second thought might say "intelligent" and "independent" instead. Their parents, she noted, took great pride in them. " 'Don't you think my Charley is a brave little fellow?' . . . 'Did you ever see such a quick eye as my Austin's?' . . . Or, if the arrow of death has stricken any of them, the stroke, the manner of it, how it was borne, and how the bereaved were sustained under it, will all be poured out. . . ."

For even after midcentury the children were still dying at a terrible rate. Three of the greatest advances in the history of medicine—anesthesia, asepsis, and pasteurization—had recently occurred, but their effects were to take years to become general. In large American cities, particularly the ports where immigrant ships arrived, infant mortality was higher than ever. In New York City in 1853, 49 percent of those who died were children under five—13 percent more than in London that same year. There was also a sudden increase in abortions. "An evil scarcely known to our fathers," lamented one New Yorker in 1857.

Early death, then, was still a common tragedy. But as Puritanism declined, there was a subtle change in the way people responded to it. As we have seen, the Puritans coped with the deaths of their children by continually reminding themselves that life was not supposed to be pleasant but was only a journey to the grave, or "an error to be rectified." No matter how beguiling a little child might be, he was only "lent," as Anne Bradstreet put it, and it was therefore foolish to become attached to him. It was better to accept what one could not change. Samuel Sewall recorded in his diary for the year 1696 the "awful yet pleasing treat" of rearranging the coffins in the Sewall family tomb.

But somewhere between 1700 and 1800, came a changing attitude toward the deaths of little children. A New England graveyard illustrates the point: seventeenth-century headstones were decorated, if at all, by a death's-head or trumpet-blowing angel ("the Trump of Doom"), whether the deceased was a child or an adult. The later graves of children were likely to bear a carved cherub, lamb, or flower to indicate that a child lay there. Still later, in the nineteenth century, this tenderness sometimes became lugubrious and morbidly sentimental. An early death came to seem romantic and almost desirable, particularly that of a beautiful young girl or handsome youth. A favorite hymn for children began with the verse:

> Youth and vigor soon will flee
> Blooming beauty lose its charm

All that's mortal soon will be
Enclosed in death's cold arms.

At sixteen, Harriet Beecher (not yet Stowe) wrote to her sister, "I don't know as I am fit for anything and I have thought that I could wish to die young and let the remembrance of me and my faults perish in the grave rather than live, as I fear I do, a trouble to everyone." There were cases of young people who seemed to "waste away" on purpose.

Children, of course, died because they had to. If a child were at death's door, all the neighbors crowded into the little sufferer's room. If any of them could compose an elegy, she (it was usually a she) did so and presented it to the parents later on black-bordered paper. Or perhaps the child himself would sing or recite an elegiac verse: "A guilty weak and helpless worm / On thy kind arm I fall" was a favorite; and, "Fresh as the grass our bodies stand / And flourish bright and gay; / A blasting wind sweeps o'er the land / And fades the grass away."

At a child's funeral in the early nineteenth century, six of the deceased's former playmates were chosen to walk beside the hearse. Even babies were put into mourning—black ribbons on a white dress—and bereaved mothers often dressed only in black for years. Little girls were put into black pantalettes. One of the functions performed by the sexton of Trinity Church, Boston— described in his memoirs *Dealings with the Dead* (1856)—was to open the coffins of children so that their mothers might gaze upon them once more. This same sexton also recalled how, as a child, he had enjoyed dropping in at Trinity when a burial was being held in the vault. He remembered the sound of shovelfuls of coarse gravel rattling down on the coffin lid, as the minister read, "Ashes to ashes, dust to dust. . . ."

There was no notion of shielding children from firsthand encounters with death (that idea is a twentieth-century one). In villages, nearly all funerals were attended by the entire citizenry, old and young. Public executions were held in many American cities until well into the nineteenth century, and it was considered morally instructive to a child to attend them. For those who missed the actual hanging, the corpse was sometimes left for weeks, decaying on the gibbet. In New Mexico, as late as the 1890s, school was let out on execution days.

Children's books were full of deathbed scenes. *Narratives of Pious Children*, one of the American Tract Society's efforts, told the story of a boy who "seemed to have the fear of God from his infancy. . . . This he manifested by frequently reproving sinners, especially his mother; telling her, that she ought not to say such bad words as she sometimes did. . . . He also reproved wicked children that were playing in the streets." All the leading characters in this book died early. "You see how happy they were when they died. . . . Do not you think that they were very good children; and do not you wish to be like them, and to die as they did?"

Better writers than the Tract Society's wrote scenes of death's parting: Harriet Beecher Stowe and her Little Eva; Louisa May Alcott and her Beth; Eugene Field and the heartrending poem about the little toy dog that was covered with dust. In fact it was very nearly impossible, until some time in the eighties, to find a book or collection of poems about or for children that did not contain at least one deathbed scene. One book that went into many editions both here and in England was *Agnes and the Key to Her Little Coffin*, written in 1857 by a New England clergyman. The book was later retitled *Agnes and the Little Key*—probably because the old-fashioned word "coffin" was going out of style in favor of "casket." Coffins, or caskets, in those days had keys (perhaps for greater security against grave robbers), and when Agnes, an eighteen-month-old baby, was buried, the undertaker gave her parents the key. They put it on a ribbon and took it out frequently to "evoke many solemn thoughts." Such as: "The key is a decoration, a badge of membership. I have a child at court [in Heaven]. She is a maid of honor." Whereas in Puritan times the dead were pictured as awaiting the Last Judgment Day before they could go to Heaven (or Hell), by the time of Agnes, people went to Heaven (or Hell) as soon as they died. Nor was there any slightest doubt as to where Agnes had gone.

Even before the new medical knowledge had begun to lower the infant mortality rate, there was considerable hue and cry in the press, calling for more to be done to promote a healthier young America. It was feared that children were being overworked in school. The Boston public schools required six hours a day in school, plus more for homework; and some boarding schools divided the day into eight hours for sleep, three for meals, two for bathing, dressing, and relaxation, and eleven for study. An article in *The Atlantic* (1859), titled "The Murder of the Innocents," reported that children were going insane from too much study. One child died "insane from sheer overwork and raving of algebra." Another prayed that she might "die and go to heaven and play with the Irish children on Saturday afternoons." A doctor at the Providence Insane Asylum was quoted as having said, "To suppose the youthful brain to be capable of the amount of work which is considered an ample allowance to an adult brain is simply absurd, and the attempt to carry this into effect must necessarily be dangerous to the health and efficacy of the organ." Another doctor decreed that children under eight should never be in school for more than four hours a day; and that if any child showed alarming symptoms of precocity he should be taken from school altogether. Not only schools but Sunday schools overworked the children, too, by holding prize competitions for learning five thousand Bible verses by heart. In defense of this practice, one Sunday school teacher remarked, "The girls would probably lose their health very soon at any rate, and may as well devote it to a sacred cause." Concluded *The Atlantic*, "[It is] our miserable ambition to have our unconscious little ones begin, in their very infancy, the race of desperate ambition which has, we admit, exhausted prematurely the lives of their parents." It was the American pattern to be worn out at an early age, "just waiting for consumption to carry them off, as one waits for the omnibus."

In a book addressed to mothers, Mrs. Sigourney chimed in. "Do not chain her to her piano, nor bow her over her book." She denounced parents who sent small children to school just to get them out of the way. One tiny girl was trudging home through the streets from school when "a pair of gay horses threw her down and a loaded sleigh passing over her literally divided her breast. She was taken up breathless, a crushed and broken flower. SHE WAS OUT OF THE WAY." And an article in *Harper's* echoed the same theme. The American girl "is a delicate plant, more exquisitely organized than the English or German, more self-relying than Italian or French, yet not generally strong in nerve and muscle, too ready to fade. . . . I have heard people say they can hardly name a single instance of perfect health among young women of their acquaintance."

But as an *Atlantic* writer pointed out in 1862, once Americans recognize that there *is* a problem, they go after it and find a solution. At the end of the fainting-spell fifties, girls began to get up from their rocking chairs and couches, loosen their stays, and open the windows. As noted earlier (in Chapter 6), it was not only a physical advantage for a young person to become proficient at a sport, but a social one. The fashion for skating, in the sixties, was followed by other sports as the century wore on: archery, croquet, lawn tennis, swimming, and bicycling. The same period saw the rise of the fashionable summer resort, where mothers and children gathered in hot weather, leaving Papa to sweat it out in the city.

At the same time, doctors were learning more and performing more effectively. J. Marion Sims (1813–1883), founder of the Woman's Hospital of the State of New York, told in his memoirs of starting out in the 1830s as a southern country doctor and of his despair at losing his first two patients, both young children. "I had not the slightest idea what to do for them," he said. The first pediatric clinic in America was established in 1862 at New York Medical College by Dr. Abraham Jacobi (1830–1919), a German immigrant who has been called the founder of American pediatrics. There were very few other such clinics until after 1900. Harvard established a chair of pediatrics in 1898.

Perhaps the most effective lifesaver for children was pasteurization. Before it was made compulsory, most city milk was hazardous, especially in warm weather. In New York, most of it came from two thousand cows kept in filthy sheds at Ninth Avenue and 18th Street, and fed on distillery waste. Milk inspection began in 1880, but not until 1930 was pasteurization required in all states.

PART THREE

The Twentieth Century

A formal portrait
Collection of the author

THE CENTURY OF
THE CHILD

THE YEAR 1900. LITTLE GIRLS WITH OUTSIZE HAIR-BOWS tying back their long curls and loose white dresses that came well below the knee; little boys in kneebritches and black stockings. Suddenly these were symbols of the twentieth century, and people were saying that this pristine new hundred years was going to be The Century of the Child; for never before in history had children been so much written about, studied, and fussed over.

As we have seen, the foregoing hundred years might well have been labeled The Century of the Mother. In 1900, Mamma was firmly entrenched as the Gentle Ruler, while Father devoted himself to business. For some time now, child-rearing advice had been written for mothers, with scant reference to the other parent. Margaret E. Sangster, in *Radiant Motherhood* (1905), makes a particular point of it: "This book is not addressed to

163

fathers. They would not have time to read it. Who ever heard of fathers in congress, conferring over the best methods of training children . . . striving to learn from one another what might best be done for the next generation?" She concedes that Father does have certain "claims," and that if he dies he is missed—but ends, "The American mother—God bless her!"

Mothers ruled their households by means of love, religion, and a mysterious and arcane faculty known as maternal instinct. According to one turn-of-the-century advisor, a mother knows instinctively whether her baby is crying in pain or because he is hungry, or simply because he wishes to be a nuisance. "It is amazing how quickly a mother learns that language. It is a mystery to most men. . . . Physicians, after experience in children's wards, understand it; and even a father, if he is patient, can acquire a moderate knowledge of it. But a mother, or even a nurse, if she is moved by a genuine maternal instinct and not by a selfish desire for her own comfort, is almost an adept at the start."

The noun *adept*, according to Webster's first definition, means an "alchemist who has attained the knowledge of how to change base metals into gold"—and indeed late-nineteenth-century mothers were supposed to possess almost magical abilities when it came to turning know-nothing little babies into noble Americans. Nevertheless, there were new forces at work in turn-of-the-century America that meant trouble for mothers who believed in their own infallible alchemy. It was a time of social reform, moral uplift, and conscientious reexamination of many heretofore unquestioned institutions. The world of children was invaded by professional child-trainers—kindergarteners, social workers, pediatricians, psychologists—people convinced they knew what they were doing according to Webster's second sense of the noun *adept*: "a highly skilled or well-trained individual: EXPERT."

Child-study groups had begun to proliferate all over the

nation in the late 1880s. The impetus was the rising prestige of science and of new ideas about education. Unlike the Mothers' Clubs of pre-Civil War days, these new organizations were not superintended by clergymen. The ladies ran them all by themselves, inviting guest lecturers who qualified as experts. Perhaps the most prestigious was Dr. L. Emmett Holt, a crusading pediatrician who came storming into the nursery to straighten out the children, especially very young babies. Dr. Holt, whose *Care and Feeding of Children* went through dozens of editions between 1894 and 1934, decreed no more coddling of babies. He was undoubtedly an influence on the lives of millions of Americans born during that time span, or more than half of those living today. Mothers who did not read child-care books were bound to hear of the Holt method from their doctors and neighbors.

There was a good deal of the Puritan in L. Emmett Holt, but he was a doctor of medicine, not divinity, and his chief interest was in physical welfare rather than spiritual. Infants, he said, must be fully regimented by the age of three or four months, eating, sleeping, and answering calls of nature according to the clock. Many earlier writers on child care had suggested that happiness came first and was more important than whether the child was dressed by eight o'clock or nine. But those writers had not been trained physicians, like Dr. Holt, whose enormous prestige with mothers was a measure of the rise of science. In millions of American homes, infants objecting to their schedules were left screaming in their cribs. Dr. Holt said it was good for them: "It is the baby's exercise." (Of course—he added casually —a sudden, sharp cry might mean scurvy or syphilis.) A really contrary infant, he warned, might try for an hour, or even for two or three hours, to get the best of his mother by crying. She must never give in, provided she is convinced that nothing is physically amiss with the child. Habitual criers should be left alone most of the time; otherwise they might become "nervous."

Babies under six months old should never be played with, and of kissing the less the better. Rocking was forbidden, and so were pacifiers. Should the child attempt to pacify himself by sucking his thumb, pasteboard splints must be applied to his elbows to prevent him from bending his arms, and at night his hands must be tied to his sides. Tots must understand that mealtime is not for fun and games. (Twenty years before, one of the unscientific experts had offered the advice, "Make the breakfast table a playground.") Mother must permit no levity at this solemn occasion, nor any playing with food, and she must see to it that children eat what is given them, and all of it. She was warned that if they ever got the notion that they could eat to please themselves, they would give trouble in other respects.

Despite the fame of Dr. Holt, one wonders how often his advice was really followed to the letter. By the early 1900s there were many new cultural patterns establishing themselves in our country, lessening the traditional force of middle-class Anglo-Saxon dicta. Anyway, the mothers belonging to that class, themselves raised by gentler methods, were likely to avoid Dr. Holt's instructions. Margaret Mead, in her memoir *Blackberry Winter*, tells us that her mother had read Holt and "accepted the admonition about never picking up a crying child unless it was in pain. But she said her babies were good babies who would cry only if something was wrong, and so she picked them up."

Dr. Holt had many followers among pediatricians who thoroughly agreed with his Spartan principles. The author of *The Training of Parents* (1900) wrote that Holt's book "ought to arrive in every household with the first-born baby or better, a few weeks in advance." The very title *The Training of Parents* was a portent: until then it was the children who were to be trained. Parents could be advised, helped, instructed, inspired, or given hints; but *trained?* Yes, it was true. The new experts were thinking up ingenious ways of hoodwinking, cajoling, or pressuring children into good behavior and these methods needed study and practice, unlike the simple old-fashioned application of the rod. There was the scorecard method, for example—a scorecard posted in the child's room and gold stars or black marks placed where it said "Rising on time," "Cleaning up room," "Writing to Grandma," and so on. Or these categories might be written on squares of paper and handed to the child before bed each evening—white squares for good behavior, blue for bad—and punishments or rewards allotted accordingly. Less doggedly methodical experts had other tactics. Mrs. Theodore W. Birney (1905) said to her little daughter, who wanted to put on her best dress to play in the yard, "Why, certainly dear, it is your dress; mother only thought she should remind her dear little girl, that there might be other afternoons when she would want it more, but mother is quite ready to fasten it for you." Mrs. Birney swore that this approach would result in the child choosing a play dress instead. To persuade a seven-year-old to stand up straight she recommended a winning smile and "What a straight manly little fellow Johnnie L is." Or, "Whenever I think you can stand, sit or walk a little straighter I will lift my eyebrows a little and smile at you and you must remind me in the same way, so that we can both be straight together."

Mrs. Burton Chance (1914) of Philadelphia admired "a blushing, shrinking child." She commended a father who told his ten-year-old daughter that the city after dark, which the child had never seen, was lit only by moon and stars. "Her ignorance of the midnight city world meant health," explained Mrs. Chance, adding that the young ought to remain "ignorant of what takes place in the world after sunset." To obtain obedience, discipline should be disguised: "Oh, my dear, you must be ill or you would never answer mother in that way. Come right up to the nursery and I will give you a dose of castor oil."

Ellen Key in 1909 advised that children should never be asked to say "I'm sorry," for this only turns them into hypocrites. "A child has a right to be naughty in peace. . . . I experience physical disgust in touching the hand of a human being that I know has struck a child." (It was Mrs. Key who popularized the phrase "The Century of the Child.") After a corporal punishment, a four-year-old child Mrs. Key knew offered the following prayer: "Dear God, tear mama's arms out so that she cannot beat me any more." Elizabeth McCracken (1913) complained of criticism from the English, who think Americans see too much of their children and treat them as friends and comrades, rendering them pert and lacking in respect. But, says Mrs. McCracken, American children are learning self-government and "to play the game." American children are good at games and enjoy playing them with adults. "Little Lord Fauntleroy . . . had acquired the habit, so characteristic of the children of our nation, of including his elders in his games." And she goes on to describe a stay in the hospital during which her room was invaded by a little girl who announced, "I came to play with you." (Presumably, Mrs. McCracken's book was not published in England.)

Before the twentieth century was many years old, Father, after at least a generation in limbo, began to be noticed again. Edgar A. Guest addressed him thus:

> Be more than his dad
> Be a chum to the lad;
> Be a part of his life
> Every hour of the day;
> Find time to talk with him
> Take time to walk with him,
> Share in his studies
> And share in his play;
> Take him to places,
> To ball games and races;
> Teach him the things
> That you want him to know.
> Don't live apart from him
> Don't keep your heart from him
> Be his best comrade
> He's needing you so.

So Dad was brought back into the picture. Not to dethrone the Gentle Ruler, of course, but as a comrade and entertainer for his children. They were to do strenuous outdoor things together —saw wood, rake leaves, hike, and camp. The idea of camping for the fun of it had come in during the eighties, and the vigorous example of President Theodore Roosevelt stimulated fathers and sons to take to the woods, where son could build a campfire and Father could build the boy's character. Nowadays there is less said about "fine character" and more about "well-adjusted personality." They used a different vocabulary fifty or sixty years ago: the word for *neurotic* was *unadjusted. Wholesome* was a favorite word—wholesome thoughts, books, food, companions, influences. And *conservation*—not in connection with birds or forests but with semen and sexual passions. These were to be conserved, lest they be used up before marriage. And it was Father's job to let his sons know. Cold baths, hard beds, and cutting down trees would prevent the boys from dwelling on the subject. "Physically fit with right personal habits for the sake of God and Country makes a splendid personal slogan for any growing boy," advised the author of *The Job of Being a Dad* (1922). In the years of the doughboy, no decent young man avoided military service. "There is no doubt about it—everybody admires a soldier. . . ." Don't wish dead soldiers alive again. "They had the best of this earth—a clean, faithful youth, a loving home, and an opportunity to give all, asking for nothing . . . and they continue, these soldier-saints, in the realm beyond. . . ."

There were scores of books like the ones we have been quoting, many of them written by scoutmasters, schoolteachers, and others who dealt professionally with the young. But let us take a look now at the contributions of those who made the study of children part of an academic discipline—the psychologists, geneticists, hereditarians, social Darwinists, and others.

For many years the one really significant name in the field of child study was that of the psychologist G. Stanley Hall. In a

Two boys, 1915
Collection of the author

brand-new field, his was the authoritative voice, although he frequently said things that laymen neither comprehended nor wanted to hear. Many of his ideas seem naive and rather bizarre today, but he was a pioneer who valiantly led the way into unknown territory.

Granville Stanley Hall was born in 1844 in a Massachusetts farming village where things had hardly changed since the previous century. All his life he looked back on his childhood there as very close to perfection—"the best educational environment for boys . . . ever realized in history," he wrote in his memoirs. Children were left much to themselves, but were constantly busy doing practical things. In the evening, by the fire, the whole family sat together with their work. Busy evenings, Hall commented, were "not so dangerous to morality." A girl might even sit in her sweetheart's lap without fear of criticism.

Hall went to Williams College and proved a brilliant student. The philanthropist Russell Sage gave him $500, enough to enable him to study in Germany for a year. After several years of teaching philosophy at Antioch, he went to Harvard and studied under William James. In those days, both philosophy and psychology were closely tied to religion; and religious principles remained part and parcel of Hall's thinking, no matter how innovative.

He evolved a theory that all children as they grow up retrace, or recapitulate, the evolution of the human race; they are born savages and gradually but surely find their way to civilization. He wrote the first scientific study of adolescents—the two-volume *Adolescence* (1904), which spoke of sex to such an extent that most librarians put it under lock and key. At that time the very word *adolescence* was not in common use, the word *youth* having formerly sufficed to cover the teen years. Hall assured parents that their adolescent sons and daughters would work their way through what might look like serious problems and come out as responsible adults. He even theorized that all adolescent boys go through a period of what he called semi-criminality.

Hall was very popular as a lecturer throughout the nineties, when mothers were banding together in child-study groups. However, when *Adolescence* was published in 1904, many parents thought it was "nasty" and turned from him. In 1910, he invited Freud, along with Ernest Jones and others of the Viennese school of psychiatry, to visit the United States. Today he is remembered for this more than for his now-outmoded theories; but at the time he earned himself nothing but disapproval. A book he published in 1913, in which he rather tentatively endorsed Freud's theories of sex in childhood, aroused great indignation, many of the reviews implying that he was nothing but a dirty old man. Bewildered and deeply hurt, he retreated to the point of ceasing to correspond with Freud and his colleagues.

He was on firm ground with the public, however, when he decreed, "we need less sentimentality and more spanking." Theodore Roosevelt, father of a large, lively family, wrote to congratulate him on this dictum. "Unless we keep the barbarian virtues, gaining the civilised ones will be of little avail," Roosevelt said. "A nation that cannot fight is not worth its salt, no matter how cultivated and refined it may be, and the very fact that it can fight often obviates the necessity of fighting. It is just so with a boy. Moreover when it comes to discipline, I cordially agree with you as to the need of physical punishment. It is not necessary often to have recourse to it, but it is absolutely necessary that the child should realize that at need it will be resorted to." Is it possible that T.R.'s diplomatic policy of "Speak softly and carry a big stick" had its origin in the Roosevelt nursery?

Hall believed that girls are so innately different from boys that there should be no coeducation after the elementary grades and that girls should be primarily educated for marriage and motherhood. ("Even the blessed mother of our Lord knew nothing of letters.") Infancy, he said, ought to be prolonged, and the teaching of reading and writing deferred until the eighth or ninth year of life, on the theory that the finger muscles are not developed until then. He thought religious doctrine was too taxing for young minds; simple Bible stories were enough until adolescence. And he advocated less pressure generally in the schools. "An ounce of health, growth, and heredity is worth a ton of education." Like the educator John Dewey, he urged the schools to permit free play rather than strictly monitored gymnastics and competitive sports, and self-expression in art rather than the kind of art class that was usual, wherein the students did nothing but copy.

Some of Hall's ideas have survived, but his theory of "recapitulation" was already out of favor by the time he died in 1924, at which time Freudianism was also much distrusted by laymen. Another of Hall's theories—the idea that heredity plays a far more important role than environment in forming a child's character—was more generally popular. It gave Nativists a reason for treating the immigrant "hordes" disdainfully; it was an excuse for not giving to charity on the grounds that to do so would be to interfere with God's plan to weed out the weak and promote the survival of the fittest. Here an old Puritan belief was ingeniously combined with Darwin's theory, the result being known as social Darwinism. (See Chapter 7 for more on this subject.)

American life changed dramatically in the years between 1910 and 1920, and with it the standards of handling children and adolescents. Perhaps the greatest single cause of the change was the automobile, which revolutionized the daily habits of families. Children could now be driven miles from home to go to school, take special lessons, or play with their peers; farm families, unless they were very isolated indeed, could easily visit the city; and teen-agers could go much farther (in two senses of the words) than they used to go with horse and buggy. Then there were the war years, and wars have always disrupted family life; but this time new responsibilities and liberty were assumed by women, who shortly thereafter got the vote. Hem lengths rose and makers of cigarettes and cosmetics experienced a boom.

And now began the great twentieth-century problem of the generation gap. The flapper appeared on the scene—a teen-age girl who ten or fifteen years before would have been just putting up her hair and lengthening her skirts nearly to the ground. She did not, however, appear out of nowhere, like Aphrodite floating in from the sea. Her older sister had prepared the way. For example, here is a 1910 description of boys and girls cavorting on a beach: "Young men in skintight, sleeveless and neckless bathing garments and . . . bare-armed girls with skirts and bloomers above the knee loll together in a sort of abandon, or dive and bathe while screaming and clutching one another like contortionists." In the opinion of the writer (Katherine Busbey, *Homes of America*), such behavior caused a girl to lose her "exquisite sex-reserve . . . the very kernel of her womanhood. When a young girl can dance and bathe and loll with only an apology for skirts with a possible or positive suitor with as little sensibility as if he were another girl, she is flouting the fundamental reason for her existence."

Mrs. Busbey was surely wrong about one thing at least—the lolling, clutching, contortionist young ladies were quite aware that their companions in the sleeveless and skintight bathing garments were not other girls. The day of the sexless cherub was gone forever and by the time the flapper arrived on the scene, most people were aware and *said* that they were aware that she had "sex appeal"—or s.a., as the polite phrase went. That was another of the changes wrought during this time—sex became mentionable. "It has struck sex o'clock in America," someone said. And although it was not until the 1970s that sex o'clock began striking as loudly as Big Ben, it all began in the early 1900s.

The problem of how to cope with adolescents became more complex, partly because young people were staying in school longer and going on to college, thus remaining dependent on their parents. (Education for girls still lagged: in 1925, the average girl left school in the ninth or tenth grade, and either worked or stayed at home helping her mother until she got married. In the upper-middle and upper classes it was not considered proper for her to work.) Most of the experts agreed that adolescence was now a more difficult period than ever: "The fires are kindled but they must be checked," said one. "Desires are awakened, but they are not to be gratified." There was too much license and petting could be a dangerous habit. Adolescents who experimented must be emotionally starved or have bad relations with their parents. Give them exhausting physical exercise, have them read uplifting authors like Tennyson and Meredith, and don't allow them any privacy. "A certain camp for boys has the commendable rule that the boys have no privacy during the entire summer." Even William Howard Taft had something to say about sex education: he was against it. "I deny," he said "that the so-called prudishness and avoidance of nasty subjects in the last generation has ever blinded any substantial number of girls or boys to the wickedness of vice or made them easier victims of temptations."

Despite President Taft, there were now more and more books on sex education—or, as one writer delicately put it, "physical aspects of the beginning of individual life." James Bigelow, who wrote extensively on the subject, stated that a girl who needed help in staying continent was either afflicted with "intensive sexuality which is often modifiable by medical or surgical treatment—or one of probably normal instincts but with radical sexual philosophy." He feared that in the future the number of such girls was likely to increase.

Where infants and young children were concerned, the mothers of the 1910s, '20s, and '30s tended to place the same

175

abiding and implicit faith in science that their grandmothers had placed in God. Quite suddenly, the name of the Deity disappeared from books and articles on child care. Instead, mothers depended on correct nutrition and scientific training in good habits. If there was an all-powerful being in the nursery it was not God but John B. Watson, Ph.D., who was not even a pediatrician but a behavioral psychologist whose special study had been monkeys and pigeons before he turned his experimental methods on the infant *homo sapiens.*

Dr. Watson's masterwork, *The Psychological Care of Infant and Child,* first appeared in 1928, but his theories were widely disseminated before that. "No one today knows enough to raise a child," he said unequivocally. "Radium has had more scientific study put upon it in the last fifteen years than has been given to the first three years of infancy since the beginning of time." And furthermore, "No mother has a right to have a child who cannot give it a room to itself for the first two years of infancy. I would make this a *conditio sine qua non.*" Having made these points (and eliminated the majority of American women from motherhood), he proceeded to lay down the law: "It is a serious question in my mind whether there should be individual homes for children—or even whether children should know their own parents. There are undoubtedly much more scientific ways of bringing up children which will probably mean finer and happier children." He feared, however, that the home was here to stay. "Even though it is proven unsuccessful, we shall always have it." Resigned to the impossibility of isolating the child from the mother or even of rotating mothers and nurses, he recommended the next best thing: cold, scientific detachment. "Never hug and kiss them, never let them sit in your lap. If you must, kiss them once on the forehead when they say good night. Shake hands with them in the morning. . . . If you expected a dog to grow up and be useful as a watchdog, a bird dog, or a fox hound . . . you wouldn't dare treat it the way you treat your child." Toddlers should be left

176

alone in the backyard during a large part of each day. They should have no toys in the bath or in bed; and of course Watson agreed with the Holt methods of clock feeding and toileting.

It was Watson's basic theory that heredity plays a minimal role in a child's character and that if he is trained like Pavlov's dog, by conditioned reflex, he will develop in any direction the parent desires. Many parents and child-care professionals greeted these ideas with enthusiasm. It sounded so easy and rational. If one could train Rover to sit up and beg, or a rose vine to climb on an arbor, then why not a human child to clean its plate and go to bed without a fuss? Conditioned reflex training! "Now we have scientific guidance," exulted the novelist Dorothy Canfield Fisher, a frequent writer on child care. The child "does what is best for him day by day not because he is beaten into it, but because it never occurs to him to do anything else." A Mrs. Thompson (*Training My Babes*, 1934) told how she conditioned her two little girls to be hungry only at mealtimes and, at the ages of two and three, to wash and dry the dishes (and none were ever broken). They went to bed with "no toys, no lights, no bottles." The only thing they might take with them was a handkerchief, but not if they were caught holding it when it was not actually in use.

One Ella Frances Lynch (1922) suggested that obedience training might begin with simple commands, as with a dog. She believed in supplementing the conditioned reflex training with a switch to the legs when instant obedience was lacking, or to correct a show of temper toward the trainer. Shortcomings such as left-handedness, thumb-sucking, and "nervousness" in general could all be controlled by her methods, she declared. It was all a matter of enforcing self-control. "Suppress the naughty wriggling!"

Watson's followers made a special point of early and strict toilet training, with the result that Watson mothers became adept at bringing baby and chamber pot together at regular intervals, day and night. "No child should be soiling diapers after he is six months old," announced the authors of *Bringing Up Your Child* (1930). If a toddler should prove recalcitrant, "make clear to him that because he has not had the desired bowel movement it will be necessary to give him medicine. I have used castor oil for this purpose because it has the taste which most children loathe most. . . . If this plan is consistently followed out, within a few days the appearance of the bottle on a table in front of the child will be an effective stimulus for the desired response in case the child has not had the bowel movement within the allotted time."

Jessica G. Cosgrave, in *The Psychology of Youth* (1929), advised mothers of small tots to sit down with a pencil and paper and make a list of good habits, and then decide which to teach first. "A good rule is to begin with each habit a few months to a year earlier than common sense would dictate." And whip the child only when it is in hysterics! If these directions are faithfully followed, then "some of the habits, which every child of fourteen should have thoroughly acquired are order, punctuality, courtesy, perseverance, cheerfulness under strain, looking for the best in others, courage under difficulties, responsibility and generosity."

To comfort parents whose toddlers became constipated or whose fourteen-year-olds broke training, the book *Wholesome Parenthood* (1929), by Ernest and Gladys Groves, took another look at Watson's theories and decided that conditioned reflex wouldn't work without motivation, and that the parent must not put faith in any sort of cut-and-dried system. Modern parents, said the authors, can't really disregard their own upbringing, but, unlike earlier generations, they often question or reject it. The result is an inconsistency that baffles children.

Many parents were exceedingly baffled, too. In their dilemma they reached out to parent-education organizations, of which there were more new ones between 1925 and 1935 than ever before. A glance at the problems they discussed and went over again and again shows that times have not changed as much as we think. Nineteen-thirties parents were concerned with movies filled with violence and sex; commercial vulgarity of various kinds; the influence of the peer group ("the child's own age group . . . may eclipse the home," wrote one advisor in 1930); the adverse effects of moving from place to place; the absent, ineffective father; inadequate schools ("our high school curricula . . . are quite hopelessly behind the modern life conditions that will have to be faced by four-fifths of the students" was a 1930 opinion); sex; rebelliousness; and, over and over, the helpless sense that "none of our old ways prepare youth."

Looking into the future
Collection of the author

10
SPOCK AND BEYOND

THAT VENERABLE CLICHÉ ABOUT THE FOREST AND THE TREES seems especially apt in describing the present world of child-rearing advice. We are in a dim and trackless forest, choked with undergrowth, and if there are any trailblazes at all, they convey only one not very helpful message: child rearing today is very difficult.

Is it really, or is this just the same old grumble that we have been hearing in this country ever since that New England minister who complained, in 1657, that the rising generation was causing him trouble and grief? Margaret Mead, for one, thinks that child rearing really is more difficult today, for the reason that children are different from any that have gone before. In her book *Culture and Commitment, A Study of the Generation Gap* (1970), Ms. Mead wrote:

> Today, nowhere in the world are there elders who know what the children know, no matter how remote and simple the societies

181

are in which the children live. In the past there were always some elders who knew more than any children in terms of their experience of having grown up within a cultural system. Today there are none. It is not only that parents are no longer guides, but that there are no guides, whether one seeks them in one's own country or abroad. There are no elders who know what those who have been reared within the last twenty years know about the world into which they were born.

Most observers hardly seem to notice that modern children are different; they are too busy commenting on—and blaming—the parents. Most parents of today's children and teen-agers were born between 1925 and 1950, and the grandparents roughly twenty-five years earlier. These generations, too, were born into a world quite different from their parents' world, and they have lived through unbelievable changes. Many things that *their* parents assured them were so have turned out not to be so. Therefore it seems small wonder that people over twenty-one are reluctant to say to children, with the giant confidence of Cotton Mather or Theodore Roosevelt, *"This is the way things are."*

And yet parents who fail to give their children the kind of firm guidance that comes from certainty are severely taken to task by nearly every child-rearing writer. Even Dr. Spock, whose tone in speaking to parents is habitually kindly and temperate, warns of the vital necessity of having convictions, ideals, and, if at all possible, religious faith. Parents, he says, must trust themselves and not become confused, even though theories of child rearing have changed so much since 1940 that "it amounts to a revolution."

Probably most of Spock's readers see common sense in what he says and if it were only theories of child raising that have changed so drastically, most of them might be able to follow his advice with no trouble. But other revolutions in our culture are what topple parental certainty. Among the more violent upheavals of the past thirty years have been: more working mothers, smaller families, "latchkey children," more divorce, smaller living quarters, the isolation of the old from the young, the Pill, greater social mobility from class to class, the decline of religion, faster and more easily available transportation, drugs, the demise of censorship, and TV.

Most child-rearing advice books published since 1940 meet the challenges of these multiple revolutions by the calm, sure method of ignoring them and handing out much of the same tried-and-true advice that has been basic for centuries. "Treat each child as an individual," for example; Anne Bradstreet, mother of eight, said that back around 1670. "Grandparents tend to be too indulgent." John Robinson noticed it at the beginning of the seventeenth century. "Children should be fed plain, wholesome food; avoid between-meal snacks." See John Locke.

And so on. No matter what the current trend, these standbys always seem worth repeating. As for trends, several have come and gone since 1940, and we can identify them by looking over the book titles before even opening the books. In 1936, heralding the end of the rigid strictness of Holt and Watson, Dr. C. Anderson Aldrich, a pediatrician, wrote *Babies Are Human Beings.* It sold very well. Some books that followed in the next few years were *In Defense of Children, Children Have Their Reasons,* and *Parents, Behave!* About the same time, the word *training* disappeared from the child-care vocabulary; it sounded like a word more suited to dogs than to human beings. (A 1930s Children's Bureau pamphlet, *Are You Training Your Child to Be Happy?,* seemed to encompass both old and new ideas.)

Between 1945 and 1955, at the height of the permissive era, there were books with titles like *Democracy in the Home, Have Fun with Your Children,* and *Stop Annoying Your Children.* In 1952, a distinguished child psychiatrist, Hilde Bruch, wrote *Don't Be Afraid of Your Child,* which blew the whistle on the more extreme permissiveness of that day, and pointed out that children had become a status and success symbol and that parent education was now a "big commodity." She doubted that parent education could be put in a capsule. "The variety of human problems is too great to be dealt with in general terms."

Nevertheless, capsules continued to be handed out, and now critics of parents who let their children bully them wrote such books as *Parents on the Run, Suburbia's Coddled Kids, The Child Worshippers, Teenage Tyranny,* and *Dangerous Fathers, Problem Mothers, and Terrible Teens.* In the last five years or so, an effort to rally parents and put new heart into them is reflected in such titles as *Parents' Effectiveness Training* and *Power to the Parents!* There have also been several books that bring up a subject the others have avoided: is it all worth it anyway? *Mother's Day Is Over* and *The Baby Trap* are two of these. They speak of the pressure from society for people to have children even though they might not want them and the difficulty of following the advice so generously ladled out.

Another way of tracing the changes in child-rearing advice is to examine the book lists of the Child Study Association since they were first compiled in 1914. In that year, the works of G. Stanley Hall dominated the list. "Character" was a word that recurred often in titles: *Principles of Character-Making, Essentials of Character.* A number of volumes were listed under the heading "Eugenics and Heredity." The words *hygiene* and *training* appeared often. The 1919 list brought a number of books on diet and nutrition (vitamins had newly been discovered). For the first time, there was a section on adolescence. In 1922, a section was added on psychology, listing books by Freud, A. A. Brill, Ernest Jones, and John B. Watson.

In 1932, the heading "Heredity and Eugenics" disappeared. New headings were "Biology, Anthropology and Genetics," "Exceptional and Unadjusted Children," and "Family Relationships." Listed under the latter was the married-sex manual *Ideal Marriage,* with the notation that it would have to be obtained "through professional sources." There were many more books on psychology than previously, including three books on mental illness, with a note reminding readers that mental illness ought to be thought of in the same light as physical illness. There were now only two books on the entire list with the word "character" in the title, and these were listed under "Philosophy, Religion and Ethics."

The latest Child Study Association book list ignores "Philosophy, Religion and Ethics" in favor of such headings as "Marriage and the Family," "Child Development," "Sex Education," and "Physical and Emotional Disability" and adds a new section covering such emergencies as divorce, death, and unstable parents.

But the important child-care book of the century is *Baby and Child Care*, by Benjamin Spock. First published in 1946 and since reprinted 179 times in paperback and many times in hardback, it has sold over 22 million copies. Although other books, before and since, have attempted to do what this book does—namely, tell parents anything they might want to know about the physical care of a child, as well as covering the emotional and disciplinary aspects of the subject—Spock, quite simply, did it better. Also his book came just at the beginning of the postwar baby boom, so that it had a wider potential market than any previous child-care book, and reached people who had never seen such a guide before. Probably because his book was so widely read, Dr. Spock has been saddled with responsibility for permissive upbringing and thus with the blame for every form of bad behavior exhibited by young people in the 1960s.

It is true that the first edition of *Baby and Child Care* appeared during the permissive trend and it does contain a few remarks that might be construed as permissive. However, much more of the book implies that the author believes in firmness, and subsequent revisions emphasize that point. If one checks out the index entries under "Discipline" one realizes that this man favors the rule of the roost by parents, not children. And his recommendations regarding teen-agers are old-fashioned—some might say outdated.

But there is a good deal of confusion in the public mind as to the proper definition of "permissiveness." Nobody ever intended it to mean license and chaos. Some parents may use it as an excuse for outright neglect or for abdication of responsibility; for others it is a well-considered plan to help a child become self-governing. Dr. Spock says, ". . . a strictness that comes from harsh feelings or a permissiveness that is timid or vacillating can each lead to poor results. The real issue is what spirit the parent puts into managing the child and what attitude is engendered in the child as a result."

One development in the field of child care that is truly unique to the twentieth century is the laboratory study of child behavior by scientists and trained professional people; not just pediatricians, psychologists, psychiatrists, and educators, as we might suppose, but by sociologists and anthropologists as well. The first child study center was the Iowa Child Welfare Research Station, established in 1917. Others followed during the 1920s and '30s, most of them attached to large universities, such as Yale, Cornell, and Minnesota. A few had an attached nursery school. (Nursery schools, which we now accept as usual for small children, date back only to 1920. Before that, for about a hundred years, small children were thought not ready to leave home; and before that, tots of an age that would now be in nursery school were sent to sit all day on hard benches and learn from an ABC that began, "With Adam's fall / We Sinn'd All.")

Besides these centers, many other types of organizations concern themselves with children and with parent education. There are thousands of parent study groups; the National Congress of Parents and Teachers has 9 million members; and there are groups run by such organizations as the Red Cross, the

Nursery school class, 1950
Collection of the author

YWCA, the General Federation of Women's Clubs, and the American Association of University Women. For years, various government agencies have published pamphlets on child-related subjects, and every ten years (since 1909) there has been a White House Conference at which, if nothing else, the experts and a good many of the would-be experts get a chance to air their views.

Research at child-study centers has resulted in far more understanding of children's problems than we have ever had before. Some of the problems we were almost unaware of previously: for example, minimal brain damage and its effect on learning ability; or the fact that some children are hypersensitive to noise or bodily contact, or are hyperactive, or need more rest than others. Teachers and parents have to learn to recognize such children, and, above all, to treat each child as a person. The Office of Child Development (a relatively recent government office, within the Department of Health, Education, and Welfare) puts out pamphlets on these subjects. It was only in the early 1940s that government pamphlets attempted to deal at all with child behavior. Before that, they limited themselves to directions for feeding and diapering and were criticized for being too adventurous when, in the 1920s, they suggested boiling the baby's milk.

The emphasis on the loving attention of a mother or of one mothering person in the early life of a baby grew out of studies made by Anna Freud with London children evacuated during the Blitz. Dr. Rene Spitz and Katherine Wolf of New York are also important figures in studies of this kind, which show that children deprived of mothering can fall into despair over its loss and become stunted not only emotionally but physically. They may even die. The famous experiments of Dr. Harry F. Harlow with monkeys showed that a motherless baby monkey, offered a choice between a dummy made of wire, equipped with milk bottles, and a dummy made of soft cloth but providing no milk, chooses the latter. Another of Dr. Harlow's experiments demonstrated that monkeys need not only early mothering but play and regular association with peers during the growing-up period.

These are among the better-known findings of the past thirty years, but there have been hundreds, and some of them concern elements never previously studied, such as the effects of genetic factors, the birth experience, viral infections, food, and "emotional atmospheres" of various kinds. Every finding is an infinitesimal piece in a tremendous puzzle. Dr. Edward Zigler, who was at the Yale Child Study Center until he became the director of the Office of Child Development, in 1970, has said, "The most intriguing questions of child development are yet to be answered."

Almost any new theory seems to provoke storms of controversy. Dr. Arnold Gesell's precise identification of stages of development, with six-month intervals in behavior change, are known far and wide, but some highly respected authorities—including Dr. Milton J. E. Senn, former director of the Yale Child Study Center—believe that Gesell and his associates were too rigid and dogmatic and that they sometimes based their conclusions on too small a sample or failed to follow through with the same children. Nevertheless, one of the great achievements of child development study is to be able to reassure parents that they can expect different responses from their children at different ages, and that seemingly inexplicable swings in behavior are perfectly normal.

Parent education is another controversial subject. A few colleges offer courses in the art (or science) of parenthood, using real babies. The Office of Child Development has tried—so far without success—to have the subject introduced into high schools, for both boys and girls. On the other hand, some prestigious doctors and educators have said that this would be a waste of good money that might better be used to train nursery-school and Head Start workers. Many people feel that Head Start does not catch children early enough and that what is needed is a Home Start program; and that what we need most is not more B.A.-degreed teachers but thousands of people specifically trained to work with babies and very young children.

It is a fact of modern life that more than 45 percent of mothers work. Yet it is only very recently that working mothers have been allowed to make income tax deductions for the cost of day care. Canada and in fact all other leading countries do more than we do for children in terms of day care centers and other support systems for families. In times gone by, day care legislation has been passed when its main purpose was to help adults, as during the Depression, when it created jobs, or as during World War II, when it freed mothers to work in factories. But there seems to be a suspicion on the part of legislators that day care is a way of helping bad mothers to avoid their responsibilities; also, that it smacks of socialism or worse. These considerations apparently mean more to them than that there are millions of young citizens without adequate care all day long and millions of "latchkey children" coming home from school every afternoon to empty houses and apartments.

The pressures on parents, as Dr. Urie Bronfenbrenner of Cornell has pointed out, make it "increasingly difficult for parents to behave as parents." In 1960 he predicted a rise in child abuse and neglect and he has been proven right. Many informed and concerned people have observed that although we claim to be a child-oriented society (and have been criticized by foreigners for it), we actually consider children's needs very little. Perhaps the fact that children are no longer needed for their labor has something to do with it; also, the fact that they are becoming more and more expensive to raise.

"I think as a culture we have not yet learned to like children," said Dr. Harold Anderson, one of the pioneers of child development study. Senator Walter F. Mondale has said that loving children is "our national myth." Dr. Edward Zigler puts it this way:

> Until there is a real awareness in this nation of the short falls . . . in respect to what we do for children, until there's a national dialogue, until there's a real sense that something is wrong and something should be done by the person in the street, I think very little is going to be done. Because the myth is still abroad in the land that this is a child-oriented society, nothing is too good for our children and they need nothing. . . . What must happen in this nation is more of an educational campaign. . . . Otherwise I think all that we're going to see is some more commissions.

He also adds, "The issue is not whether we're going to have more day care . . . but rather what quality is it going to be?" And, finally (Dr. Zigler quit his job as director of the Office of Child Development, thoroughly frustrated), "Children's programs are in the hands of bureaucrats who might as well be at the post office."

Another subject that has only recently been seriously considered is that of children's rights. What are the rights of children, and are children getting what they are legally and morally entitled to? Nothing in the Constitution gives them specific protection. The Bill of Rights was meant for white adult males. The Fourteenth Amendment extended this protection to black adult males and the Nineteenth Amendment to adult females. But children are not mentioned. They cannot sue and they are much more restricted in their freedoms than adults. For example, a child runaway from home or truant from school is liable to arrest, no matter what abuse or neglect he may have been suffering. A child who commits a petty crime may be kept in custody for years, while an adult, committing the same crime, gets off with a fine or a short term in the workhouse. Sometimes parents of children who have committed no crime but are stubborn and hard to handle bring them to juvenile court; the judge has no other recourse than to throw such children in with other juveniles, many of whom may be guilty of major crimes or who may be the worst possible company for a troubled child. Of late, a new and frightening development further complicates the world of child crime and punishment: more and more serious crimes are being committed by younger and younger children who must be turned back on the streets because the facilities for dealing with them are inadequate.

Protecting the rights of children is intricate and tricky. Proposals have been made for the appointment of child advocates who would defend children in court without any ties to parents, educators, or judges. A cabinet office, "Secretary for Children," is another idea; or a children's advocate in the White House; or a civil agency to help nondelinquent minors for whom the parent-child relationship has broken down. Not long ago, Senators Mondale and Ribicoff sponsored a bill to establish child advocates, but it was roundly defeated. It looked too much like an invasion of the authority of parents and teachers, most of whom feel they have enough trouble as it is; also, it was feared to be just one more governmental infringement of individual rights, one more increase in government spending, and one more swelling of the bureaucracy.

Perhaps none of the schemes so far proposed is workable, but the fact remains that the radical changes in modern life seem to call for radical changes in our thinking about children. In proposing his bill, Senator Mondale pointed out that business can write off the expenses of jet planes and entertainment, but the average family gets only a small income tax deduction for the expenses of child raising—which, according to the latest estimates, costs between $40,000 and $75,000 per child from birth through college.

The Supreme Court recently ruled that children are "persons." Perhaps we are moving ahead.

Bibliography

GENERAL BACKGROUND

Aries, Philippe. *The Centuries of Childhood.* New York, 1962.

Banks, Louis Albert. *Youth of Famous Americans.* Cincinnati, 1902.

Bremner, Robert H., ed. *Children and Youth in America,* 3 vols. Cambridge, Mass., 1970–74.

Brim, Orville. *Education for Child Rearing.* New York, 1959.

Campbell, Mildred. *The English Yeoman.* New Haven, 1942.

Field, E. M. *The Child and His Book.* London, 1891.

Goodsell, Willystine. *Problems of the Family.* New York, 1928.

Greven, Philip J., Jr., ed. *Child-Raising Concepts, 1628–1861.* Itasca, Ill., 1973.

Hall, Thomas C. *The Religious Background of American Culture.* New York, 1930.

Halsey, Rosalie V. *Forgotten Books of the American Nursery.* Boston, 1911.

Hendrickson, Norejane Johnston. *A Brief History of Parent Education in the United States.* Columbus, Ohio, 1963.

King-Hall, Magdalen. *The Story of the Nursery.* London, 1958.

Laslett, Peter. *The World We Have Lost.* New York, 1965.

McClinton, Katharine Morrison. *Antiques of American Childhood.* New York, 1970.

Notestein, Wallace. *The English People on the Eve of Colonization.* New York, 1954.

Ritchie, Oscar W., and Koeler, Marvin R. *Sociology of Childhood.* New York, 1964.

Sears, Robert, et al. *Patterns of Child Rearing.* Evanston, Ill., 1957.

Smith, Elva S. *A History of Children's Literature.* Chicago, 1937.

CHAPTERS I AND 2

Adams, Abigail. *Letters.* Boston, 1848.

———. *New Letters.* Boston, 1947.

Anburey, Thomas. *Travels through the Interior Parts of America.* Boston, 1923.

Bliss, William Root. *Side Glimpses from the Colonial Meeting-House.* Boston, 1894.

Bradstreet, Anne. *Works.* New York, 1932.

Brenner, Scott Francis. *Pennsylvania Dutch.* Harrisburg, Pa., 1957.

Bruce, Philip Alexander. *The Social Life of Virginia in the Seventeenth Century.* New York, 1964.

Burnaby, Andrew. *Travels through North America.* London, 1775.

Chastellux, Marquis de. *Travels in North America.* Chapel Hill, 1963.

Clark, Imogen. *Old Days and Old Ways.* New York, 1928.

Crouch, Nathaniel. *Youth's Divine Pastime.* Boston, 1749.

Dayton, Abram. *The Last Days of Knickerbocker Life.* New York, 1880.

Eames, Wilberforce. *Early New England Catechisms.* Worcester, Mass., 1898.

Earle, Alice Morse. *Child Life in Colonial Days.* New York, 1899.

———. *Home Life in Colonial Days.* New York, 1913.

Edwards, Jonathan. *A Faithful Narrative of the Surprising Work of God . . . at Northampton.* 1736.

Fiske, John. *The Dutch and Quaker Colonies in America*, 2 vols. Boston, 1899.

Fithian, Philip Vickers. *Journal and Letters.* Williamsburg, 1957.

Fleming, Sandford. *Children and Puritanism.* New Haven, 1933.

Ford, Paul Leicester. *The New England Primer.* New York, 1897.

Franklin, Benjamin. *Autobiography.* New York, 1959.

Grant, Mrs. Anne. *Memoirs of an American Lady.* New York, 1901.

Hanscom, Elizabeth Deering. *The Heart of the Puritan.* New York, 1917.

Hart, Albert Bushnell, ed. *Colonial Children.* New York, 1902.

Holliday, Carl. *Woman's Life in Colonial Days.* Boston, 1922.

Huntington, Arria S. *Under a Colonial Roof.* Boston, 1891.

Ironside, Charles E. *The Family in Colonial New York.* New York, 1942.

Janeway, James. *A Token for Children, being an Exact Account of the Conversion, Holy and Exemplary Lives and Joyful Deaths of Several Young Children.* Boston, 1775.

Lawrence, Henry W. *The Not-Quite Puritans.* Boston, 1928.

Locke, John. *Some Thoughts Concerning Education.* London, 1695.

MacElroy, Mary Holbrook. *Work and Play in Colonial Days.* New York, 1917.

Mather, Cotton. *Corderius Americanus.* Boston, 1708.

———. *Diary.* New York, 1967.

———. *Early Piety—Exemplified in the Life and Death of Mr. Nathaniel Mather.* Boston, 1857.

BIBLIOGRAPHY

Mather, Cotton. *A Family Well Ordered.* Boston, 1699.
Morgan, Edmund. *The Gentle Puritan.* New Haven, 1962.
———. *The Puritan Dilemma.* Boston, 1958.
———. *The Puritan Family.* Boston, 1944.
———. *Virginians at Home.* Williamsburg, 1952.
Morison, Samuel Eliot. *Harvard in the Seventeenth Century.* Cambridge, Mass., 1936.
———. *Three Centuries of Harvard.* Cambridge, Mass., 1936.
The New Gift for Children. Boston, 1762.
Nurse Truelove. Worcester, Mass., 1786.
Quincy, Eliza Susan Morton. *Diary.* Boston, 1861.
Robinson, John. *New Essays.* N.p., 1628.
Rosenbach, Dr. J. *Early American Children's Books.* New York, 1933.
Rowse, A. L. *The England of Elizabeth.* New York, 1950.
Scudder, H. E. *Men and Manners in America.* New York, 1887.
Sewall, Samuel. *Diary.* New York, 1974.
Seybolt, Robert Francis. *Apprenticeship and Apprenticeship Education in Colonial New England and New York.* New York, 1917.
Sherrill, Charles H., ed. *French Memoirs of Eighteenth-Century America.* New York, 1915.
Singleton, Esther. *Dutch New York.* New York, 1909.
———. *Social Life under the Georges.* New York, 1902.
Sloane, William. *Children's Books in England and America in the Seventeenth Century.* New York, 1955.
Smith, Abbot Emerson. *Colonists in Bondage.* Chapel Hill, 1947.
Smith, James Morton, ed. *Seventeenth Century America.* Chapel Hill, 1959.
Spruill, Julia Cherry. *Women's Life and Work in the Southern Colonies.* New York, 1938.
Stiles, Henry Reed. *Bundling.* Albany, 1871.
Taylor, William R. *Cavalier and Yankee.* New York, 1961.
Vanderbilt, Gertrude. *Social History of Flatbush.* New York, 1881.
Wadsworth, Benjamin, et al. *A Course of Sermons on Early Piety.* Boston, 1721.
Wigglesworth, Michael. *The Day of Doom.* New York, 1929.
Winslow, Anna Green. *Diary of a Boston School Girl.* Boston, 1894.
Winslow, Ola E. *Jonathan Edwards.* New York, 1940.
Winsor, Justin, ed. *Memorial History of Boston,* 4 vols. Boston, 1881.
Wright, Louis B. *Everyday Life in Colonial America.* New York, 1965.
Ziff, Larzer. *Puritanism in America.* New York, 1973.

CHAPTER 3

Armes, Ethel, ed. *Nancy Shippen, Her Journal Book*. Philadelphia, 1935.

Armstrong, Margaret. *Five Generations*. New York, 1930.

Arnold, Samuel. *An Astonishing Affair*. Concord, N.H., 1830.

Barbauld, Mrs. *Lessons for Children from Two to Four*. Philadelphia, 1788.

Bernard, John. *Retrospections of America, 1797–1811*. New York, 1887.

Bowne, Eliza Southgate. *A Girl's Life Eighty Years Ago*. New York, 1887.

Comstock, Cyrus. *Essays on the Duty of Parents and Children*. Hartford, 1810.

D'Arusmont, Frances Wright. *Society and Manners in America*. London, 1821.

de Warville, Brissot. *New Travels in the United States of America*. Cambridge, Mass., 1964.

Dwight, Theodore. *Sketches of Scenery and Manners in the United States*. New York, 1829.

Edel, Leon. *Henry James: The Untried Years, 1843–1870*. Philadelphia, 1953.

Foster, Sir Augustus John. *Notes on the United States of America, Collected in the Years 1805-6-7, and 1811-12*. San Marino, Calif., 1954.

Griffith, E. *Letters Addressed to Young Married Women*. Philadelphia, 1796.

Hall, Basil. *Travels in North America*. London, 1828.

Hitchcock, Enos. *Memoirs of the Bloomsgrove Family*, 2 vols. Boston, 1790.

Hoare, Mrs. Louisa. *Hints for the Improvement of Early Education and Nursery Discipline*. New York, 1820.

Juvenile Miscellany. Philadelphia, 1808.

Leslie, Eliza. *American Girl's Book, or Occupation for Play Hours*. Boston, 1831.

Lewis, Taylor. *My Old Schoolmaster*. Schenectady, N.Y., 1874.

Little Truths containing Information on divers Subjects for the Instruction of Children. Boston, 1794.

MacElroy, Mary H. *Work and Play in Colonial Days*. New York, 1917.

My Mother's Grave. New York, 1830.

Pond, Enoch. *Autobiography*. Boston, 1884.

A Pretty New Year's Gift. Worcester, Mass., 1796.

Taylor, Jane. *Rhymes for the Nursery*. Boston, 1837.

Tuckerman, Joseph. *A Word to Fathers and Mothers*. Boston, 1828.

van Doren, Mark, ed. *Correspondence of Aaron Burr and His Daughter Theodosia*. New York, 1929.

BIBLIOGRAPHY

Weed, Enos. *Educational Directory.* Newark, 1803.
Wishy, Bernard. *The Child and the Republic.* Philadelphia, 1968.
Witherspoon, John. *Letters on Education.* New York, 1815.

CHAPTER 4

Adams, Henry. *John Randolph.* Boston, 1895.
Alston, J. Motte. *Rice Planter and Sportsman.* Columbia, S.C., 1953.
Armstrong, Orland Kay. *Old Massa's People.* Indianapolis, 1931.
Banks, Mary Ross. *Bright Days in Old Plantation Times.* Boston, 1882.
Blackford, John. *Ferry Hill Plantation Journal.* Chapel Hill, 1961.
Botkin, B. A., ed. *Lay My Burden Down.* Chicago, 1945.
Bowers, Claude. *The Young Jefferson.* Boston, 1945.
Bruce, W. C. *John Randolph of Roanoke.* New York, 1922.
Buckingham, James Silk. *The Slave States of America,* 2 vols. London, 1842.
Burge, Dolly. *Diary.* Athens, Ga., 1962.
Burke, Emily P. *Reminiscences of Georgia.* Oberlin, Ohio, 1850.
Burwell, Letitia M. *A Girl's Life in Virginia.*
Chamberlain, Hope Summerell. *Old Days in Chapel Hill.* Chapel Hill, n.d.
Chesnut, Mary Boykin. *A Diary From Dixie.* Boston, 1949.
Coleman, J. Winston, Jr. *Slavery Times in Kentucky.* Chapel Hill, 1940.
Davis, Edwin A., ed. *Plantation Life in the Florida Parishes of Louisiana 1836–46, as Reflected in the Diary of Bennet H. Barrow.* New York, 1943.
De Saussure, Nancy. *Old Plantation Days.* New York, 1909.
Dew, Thomas R. *An Essay on Slavery.* N.p., 1849.
Frémont, Jessie Benton. *Souvenirs of My Time.* Boston, 1887.
Gregory, John. *A Father's Legacy to His Daughter.* London, 1828.
Hundley, Daniel R. *Social Relations in Our Southern States.* New York, 1860.
Janson, Charles William. *The Stranger in America, 1793–1806.* New York, 1935.
Johnson, Charles S. *Shadow of the Plantation.* Chicago, 1934.
Johnson, Guion Griffis. *A Social History of the Sea Islands.* Chapel Hill, 1930.
Lerner, Gerda. *The Grimké Sisters.* Boston, 1967.
Mallard, R. Q. *Plantation Life before Emancipation.* Richmond, 1892.
McElroy, Robert. *Jefferson Davis.* New York, 1937.

Merrick, Caroline E. *Old Times in Dixieland.* New York, 1901.
Myers, Robert Manson, ed. *The Children of Pride.* New Haven, 1972.
Page, Thomas Nelson. *Social Life in Old Virginia.* New York, 1900.
Prewrie, Louise Clark. *Diddy, Dumps and Tot.* New York, 1882.
Pryor, Mrs. Roger. *My Day.* New York, 1909.
Ripley, Elizabeth Moore. *Social Life in Old New Orleans.* New York, 1912.
Robertson, Douglas S., ed. *Joseph Hadfield's Diary.* Toronto, 1933.
Russell, Phillips. *The Woman Who Rang the Bell.* Chapel Hill, 1949.
Smedes, Susan Dabney. *Memorials of a Southern Planter.* New York, 1965.
Smyth, John F. D. *A Tour in the United States of America.* London, 1784.
Stampp, Kenneth M. *The Peculiar Institution.* London, 1964.
Warren, Edward. *A Doctor's Experiences on Three Continents.* Baltimore, 1885.

CHAPTERS 5–8

Abbott, Edith. *Some American Pioneers in Social Welfare.* Chicago, 1937.
Abbott, Eleanor H. *Being Little in Cambridge.* New York, 1936.
Abbott, Grace. *The Child and the State,* 2 vols. New York, 1938.
Abbott, Jacob. *Gentle Measures in the Management of the Young.* New York, 1899.
Abbott, John. *The Mother at Home.* New York, 1833.
Adams, Nehemiah. *Agnes and the Key to Her Little Coffin.* Boston, 1857.
Adamson, William R. *Bushnell Rediscovered.* Philadelphia, 1966.
Alcott, Louisa May. *Eight Cousins.* Boston, 1875.
———. *Spinning Wheel Stories.* Boston, 1884.
Alcott, William. *Forty Years in the Wilderness of Pills and Powders.* Boston, 1859.
———. *Letters to a Sister.* Buffalo, 1850.
———. *A Young Man's Guide.* Boston, 1840.
———. *The Young Mother.* Boston, 1836.
Aldrich, Auretta Reys. *Children, Their Models and Critics.* New York, 1892.
Aldrich, Dr. F. L. S. *My Child and I.* Philadelphia, 1903.
Allen, Elizabeth Akers. *Rock Me to Sleep, Mother.* Boston, 1883.
American Lady's Medical Pocket-Book and Nursery-Adviser. Philadelphia, 1833.
Arey, Mrs. H. E. G. *Home and School Training.* Philadelphia, 1884.
Aveling, Edward. *An American Journey.* New York, 1887.
Balsan, Consuelo Vanderbilt. *The Glitter and the Gold.* New York, 1952.

BIBLIOGRAPHY

Barrett, Maria. *Looking Back from Eighty-Five.* Chicago, 1926.

Baxter, William Edward. *America and the Americans.* London, 1855.

Beadle, Charles. *A Trip to the United States in 1887.* London, 1888.

Bennett, Mary E. [Elizabeth Glover]. *The Children's Wing.* New York, 1889.

Bigelow, Maurice A. *Sex-education.* New York, 1936.

Bird, Isabella. *An Englishwoman in America.* London, 1856.

Blake, May. *26 Hours a Day.* Boston, 1883.

Blum, John Morton, ed. *Yesterday's Children.* Boston, 1959.

Bookwalter, L. *The Family, or the Home and the Training of Children.* Dayton, Ohio, 1894.

Bowen, Louise de Koven. *Growing Up with a City.* New York, 1926.

Breck, Samuel. *Recollections.* Philadelphia, 1877.

Brigham, Amariah. *Remarks on the Influence of Mental Cultivation and Mental Excitement in Health.* Boston, 1833.

Burney, Mrs. Theodore. *Childhood.* New York, 1905.

Burton, Warren. *Helps to Education.* Boston, 1863.

Canby, Henry Seidel. *The Age of Confidence.* New York, 1934.

Caulfield, Ernest. *The Infant Welfare Movement in the Eighteenth Century.* New York, 1831.

Chase, Mary Ellen. *A Goodly Heritage.* New York, 1932.

Cheley, Frank H. *The Job of Being a Dad.* Boston, 1923.

Child, Frank. *The Colonial Parson of New England.* New York, 1896.

Child, Lydia. *The Mother's Book.* Boston, 1844.

Clark, Orange. *A Discourse on Family Discipline.* New York, 1860.

Combe, George. *Tour in the United States.* Philadelphia, 1841.

Coxe, Maria. *The Young Lady's Companion.* Gambia, Ohio, 1839.

Crepeau, Henry J. *Rhode Island: A History of Child Welfare Planning.* Washington, D.C., 1941.

Cross, Barbara M. *Horace Bushnell.* Chicago, 1958.

Dewees, William P. *A Treatise on the Physical and Medical Treatment of Children.* Philadelphia, 1838.

Dickens, Charles. *American Notes.* London, 1843.

Drake, Emma F. Angell. *What a Young Wife Ought to Know.* Philadelphia, 1901.

Drinker, Elizabeth. *Extracts from the Journal of Elizabeth Drinker.* Philadelphia, 1889.

Duncan, Mary. *America as I Found It.* New York, 1852.

Dwight, Theodore, Jr. *The Father's Book.* Springfield, Mass., 1834.

Faithfull, Emily. *Three Visits to America.* Edinburgh, 1884.

Ferguson, William. *America by River and Rail.* London, 1855.

Fosdick, Raymond. *John D. Rockefeller, Jr.: A Portrait.* New York, 1956.

Furness, Clifton J. *The Genteel Female.* New York, 1931.

Gilman, Stella. *Mothers in Council.* New York, 1884.

Goodrich, S. G. [Peter Parley]. *Recollections of a Lifetime.* New York, 1857.

Gouverneur, Marian. *As I Remember.* New York, 1911.

Grinnell, Elizabeth. *How John and I Brought Up the Child.* Philadelphia, 1894.

Grund, Francis J. *The Americans in Their Moral, Social and Political Relations.* London, 1837.

Haines, T. L. *Worth and Wealth.* New York, 1883.

Hall, Florence Howe. *Social Customs.* New York, 1887.

Hall, G. Stanley. *Adolescence,* 2 vols. New York, 1904.

Hall, Jeannette Winter. *Life's Story.* La Crosse, Wisc., 1911.

Hall, Winfield. *John's Vacation.* Chicago, 1913.

Harris, Mrs. F. McCready. *Plain Talks with Young Homemakers.* Rahway, N.J., 1889.

Harris, Walter. *A Treatise of the Acute Diseases of Children.* London, 1742.

Hawthorne, Julian. *Memoirs.* New York, 1938.

Hawthorne, Nathaniel. *American Notebooks.* New Haven, 1932.

Hendley, George. *Narratives of Pious Children.* New York, n.d.

Henry, Mrs. S. M. I. *Studies in Home and Child Life.* New York, 1897.

Hersey, John. *Advice to Christian Parents.* Baltimore, n.d.

Higginson, Thomas Wentworth. *Cheerful Yesterdays.* Boston, 1898.

Hone, Philip. *Diary.* New York, 1927.

Hopkinson, Mrs. C. A. *Hints for the Nursery.* Boston, 1863.

Hyde, Alvan. *Essay on the State of Infants.* New York, 1830.

Jackson, James. *Training of Children.* Dansville, N.Y., 1872.

Jordan, Alice. *From Rollo to Tom Sawyer.* Boston, 1948.

Kuhn, Anne L. *The Mother's Role in Childhood Education: New England Concepts, 1830–1860.* New Haven, 1947.

The Ladies' Indispensable Assistant. New York, 1851.

Larcom, Lucy. *A New England Girlhood.* Boston, 1889.

Laurie, J. *Parent's Guide.* Philadelphia, 1854.

Leeds, Daniel. *Almanac.* New York, 1705.

LeFavre, Carrica. *Mother's Help and Child's Best Friend.* New York, 1890.

Levinson, Abraham. *Pioneers of Pediatrics.* New York, 1936.

Lodge, Henry Cabot. *Early Memories.* Boston, 1913.

MacCracken, Henry Noble. *The Family on Gramercy Park.* New York, 1949.

Marryat, Captain. *Diary in America.* Bloomington, Ind., 1960.

Martineau, Harriet. *Society in America.* Paris, 1842.

Mavor, William. *The Catechism of Health.* New York, 1819.

Mennel, Robert M. *Thorns and Thistles.* Durham, N.H., 1973.

Meye, Ernst. *Infant Mortality in New York City.* New York, 1921.

Moll, Albert. *The Sexual Life of the Child.* New York, 1912.

Morley, Margaret Warner. *The Renewal of Life.* Chicago, 1906.

———. *A Song of Life.* Chicago, 1909.

Murray, Hon. Amelia M. *Letters.* New York, 1856.

Murray, Maude C. *Child Life: Physical and Mental Development.* New York, 1895.

Murray, Nicholas ["Kirwan"]. *Happy Home.* New York, 1858.

Neumann, Henry. *Modern Youth and Marriage.* New York, 1928.

Porter, Ann E. *Uncle Jerry's Letters to Young Mothers.* Boston, 1854.

Porter, Henry H. *Catechism of Health.* Philadelphia, 1831.

Pratt, Samuel W. *A Summer at Peace Cottage.* New York, 1880.

Reese, D. Meredith. *Report on Infant Mortality in Large Cities.* Philadelphia, 1857.

Richards, Caroline Cowles. *Village Life in America.* New York, 1908.

Richmond, Winifred. *The Adolescent Girl.* New York, 1925.

Riis, Jacob. *How the Other Half Lives.* New York, 1900.

Rowe, Stuart H. *The Physical Nature of the Child.* New York, 1903.

Sala, George. *America Revisited.* London, 1885.

Sangster, Margaret E. *Hours with Girls.* New York, 1881.

———. *Radiant Motherhood.* New York, 1909.

Sargent, Lucius Manlius. *Dealings with the Dead.* Boston, 1856.

Sedgwick, Catharine. *Facts and Fancies for School-Day Reading.* New York, 1848.

———. *Means and Ends, or Self-Training.* Boston, 1839.

———. *Morals of Manners.* Boston, 1846.

Sherwood, M. E. W. *An Epistle to Posterity.* New York, 1897.

Sigourney, Lydia H. *Letters to Mothers.* Hartford, 1838.

———. *Sayings of Little Ones.* New York, 1854.

Sims, J. Marion. *The Story of My Life.* New York, 1884.

Smith, Hannah Whitall. *The Science of Motherhood.* New York, 1894.

Social Etiquette of New York. New York, 1887.

Sperry, Lyman Beecher. *Confidential Talks with Young Women.* Chicago, 1893.

Stall, Sylvanus. *Successful Selling of the Self and Sex Series.* Philadelphia, 1907.

Stall, Sylvanus. *What Parents Should Teach Their Children.* Philadelphia, 1912.
———. *What a Young Boy Ought to Know.* Philadelphia, 1936.
Still, George Frederic. *The History of Pediatrics.* London, 1931.
Stowe, Harriet Beecher, and Beecher, Catharine E. *The American Woman's Home.* New York, 1869.
Sullivan, Edward. *Rambles and Scrambles in North and South America.* London, 1852.
Taylor, T. W. *Home Health and Happiness.* Indianapolis, 1887.
Thrailkill, John W. *An Essay on the Causes of Infant Mortality.* St. Louis, 1869.
Tomes, Robert. *The Bazar Book of Decorum.* New York, 1870.
———. *The Bazar Book of the Household.* New York, 1875.
———. *Youth's Health Book.* New York, 1877.
Towle, George Makepeace. *American Society.* London, 1872.
Trippe, Mrs. Mattie W. *Home Treatment for Children.* Chicago, 1881.
Trollope, Anthony. *Travels in North America.* New York, 1863.
Underwood, Michael. *A Treatise on the Diseases of Children.* Philadelphia, 1793.
van Rensselaer, Mrs. John King. *The Social Ladder.* New York, 1924.
van Wyck, Frederick. *Recollections of an Old New Yorker.* New York, 1932.
Welsh, Sister Mary Michael. *Catharine Maria Sedgwick.* Washington, D.C., 1937.
Wiggin, Kate Douglas. *Children's Rights.* Boston, 1892.
———. *The Woman's Book.* New York, 1894.
Willis, N. P. *The Rag-bag.* New York, 1855.
Winterburn, Florence Hull. *Nursery Ethics.* New York, 1895.
Wortley, Lady Emmeline. *Travels in the United States.* London, 1851.
Wyllie, Irwin. *The Selfmade Man in America.* New York, 1954.

CHAPTERS 9 AND 10

Adams, Grace. *Your Child Is Normal.* New York, 1934.
Aldrich, C. Anderson. *Babies Are Human Beings.* New York, 1936.
Alschuler, Rose H., et al. *Two to Six.* New York, 1937.
Anderson, Harold H. *Children in the Family.* New York, 1937.
Anderson, John. *The Young Child in the Home.* New York, 1936.
Bacmeister, Rhoda W. *All in the Family.* New York, 1951.
Baker, Edna Dean. *Parenthood and Child Nurture.* New York, 1922.

Beasley, Christine. *Democracy in the Home.* New York, 1954.

Beck, Joan. *How to Raise a Brighter Child.* New York, 1967.

Bernhardt, Karl S. *Discipline and Child Guidance.* New York, 1964.

Betts, George Herbert. *Fathers and Mothers.* Indianapolis, 1915.

Beverly, Bert I. *In Defense of Children.* New York, 1941.

Bird, Joseph, and Bird, Lois. *Power to the Parents!* New York, 1972.

Birney, Mrs. Theodore W. *Childhood.* New York, 1905.

Black, Irma Simonton. *Off to a Good Start.* New York, 1941.

Blaine, Graham B., Jr. *Are Parents Bad for Children?* New York, 1973.

Blatz, William E., and Bolt, Helen. *The Management of Young Children.* New York, 1930.

Bowlby, John, et al. *Maternal Care and Mental Health.* New York, 1951.

Bressler, Leo, and Bressler, Marion. *Youth in American Life.* Boston, 1972.

Bricklin, Barry, and Bricklin, Patricia M. *Strong Family—Strong Child.* New York, 1970.

Brill, Alice C., and Youtz, May Pardee. *Your Child and His Parents.* New York, 1932.

Bronfenbrenner, Urie. *Two Worlds of Childhood.* New York, 1970.

Bruce, H. Addington. *Psychology and Parenthood.* New York, 1915.

Bruch, Hilde. *Don't Be Afraid of Your Child.* New York, 1952.

Burrell, Caroline Benedict, and Forbush, William Byron. *Manual for Character Training.* New York, 1915.

———. *The Mother's Book.* New York, 1919.

Busbey, Katherine. *Homes of America.* London, 1910.

Cavan, Ruth Shonle. *The American Family.* New York, 1963.

Chance, Mrs. Burton. *Self-Training for Mothers.* Philadelphia, 1914.

Chapin, Henry D. *Heredity and Child Culture.* New York, 1922.

Chapman, A. H. *A Guide for Perplexed Parents.* Philadelphia, 1966.

Chenery, Susan. *As the Twig Is Bent.* Boston, 1901.

Chess, Stella; Thomas, Alexander; and Buch, Herbert G. *Your Child Is a Person.* New York, 1965.

Cobb, Stanwood. *New Horizons for the Child.* Washington, D.C., 1934.

Cosgrave, Jessica G. *The Psychology of Youth.* New York, 1929.

Cowan, Edwina A., and Carlson, Avis D. *Bringing Up Your Child.* Duffield, N.Y., 1930.

Craig, Sidney D. *Raising Your Child, Not by Force but by Love.* Philadelphia, 1973.

Davis, W. Allison, and Hanghurst, Robert J. *Father of the Man.* Boston, 1947.

Dittmann, Laura L., ed. *Early Child Care.* New York, 1968.

Dodson, Fitzhugh. *How to Parent.* New York, 1971.

Drury, Samuel S. *Backbone.* New York, 1923.

Duffus, R. L., and Holt, L. Emmett, Jr. *L. Emmett Holt.* New York, 1940.

Ehrmann, Winston. *Premarital Dating Behavior.* New York, 1959.

Erikson, Erik H. *Childhood and Society.* New York, 1963.

———. *Identity, Youth and Crisis.* New York, 1968.

Farber, Seymour M., and Wilson, Roger H. L., eds. *Teen Age Marriage and Divorce.* Berkeley, 1967.

Fishbein, Morris L., ed. *Modern Marriage and Family Living.* New York, 1957.

Fisher, Dorothy Canfield. *What Grandmother Did Not Know.* Boston, 1922.

——— and Gruenberg, Sidonie M. *Our Children: A Handbook for Parents.* New York, 1932.

Forbush, William B. *The Boy Problem.* Boston, 1901.

———. *The Government of Adolescent Young People.* Boston, 1913.

Forman, Henry James. *Our Movie Made Children.* New York, 1933.

Foster, Geraldine B. *The Best Method of Raising Children.* Philadelphia, 1924.

Fraiberg, Selma H. *The Magic Years.* New York, 1959.

Garland, Joseph. *The Road to Adolescence.* Cambridge, Mass., 1934.

Gilbert, Dan. *The Slaughter of Innocence.* San Diego, 1937.

Ginott, Haim. *Between Parent and Child.* New York, 1955.

———. *Between Parent and Teenager.* New York, 1969.

Glover, Katherine, and Dewey, Evelyn. *Children of the New Day.* New York, 1934.

Goodspeed, Helen, and Johnson, Emma. *Care and Training of Children.* Philadelphia, 1929.

Goodspeed, Helen; Mason, Esther R.; and Woods, Elizabeth L. *Child Care and Guidance.* Philadelphia, 1948.

Gorer, Geoffrey. *The American People.* New York, 1948.

Gottlieb, David, ed. *Children's Liberation.* Englewood Cliffs, N.J., 1973.

Groves, Ernest, and Groves, Gladys. *Wholesome Parenthood.* New York, 1929.

Gruenberg, Sidonie M. *Our Children Today.* New York, 1952.

———. *Sons and Daughters.* New York, 1916.

———. "Then and Now." New York, 1952. (Pamphlet)

Hale, Nathan G., Jr. *Freud and the American.* Oxford, 1971.

Hall, G. Stanley, et al. *Aspects of Child Life and Education.* New York, 1921.

BIBLIOGRAPHY

Handlin, Oscar, and Handlin, Mary F. *Facing Life: Youth and the Family in American History*. Boston, 1971.

Hawes, Joseph M. *Children in Urban Society*. New York, 1971.

Henry, Katherine. *Back Home in Pennsylvania*. Philadelphia, 1917.

Holt, L. Emmett. *Care and Feeding of Children*. New York, 1934.

Horwich, Frances, and Werrenrath, Reinald, Jr. *Have Fun with Your Children*. New York, 1954.

Hurlock, Elizabeth. *Modern Ways with Children*. New York, 1943.

Hurt, H. W. *The Child and His Home*. New York, 1931.

Ilg, Frances L., and Ames, Louise Bates. *The Gesell Institute's Child Behavior*. New York, 1958.

Jackson, Gabrielle E. *Don'ts for Mothers*. Boston, 1903.

Josselyn, Irene Milliken. *The Happy Child*. New York, 1955.

Kagan, Jerome, and Coles, Robert, eds. *Twelve to Sixteen: Early Adolescence*. New York, 1971.

Kanner, Leo. *In Defense of Mothers*. New York, 1941.

Key, Ellen. *The Education of the Child*. New York, 1909.

Kugelmass, I. Newton. *Growing Superior Children*. New York, 1937.

LeMasters, E. E. *Parents in Modern America*. Homewood, Ill., 1970.

Levinson, Abraham. *Pioneers of Pediatrics*. New York, 1936.

Lynch, Ella Frances. *Bookless Lessons for the Teacher-Mother*. New York, 1922.

Madsen, Clifford K., and Madsen, Charles H., Jr. *Parents, Children, Discipline*. Boston, 1972.

Marney, Carlyle. *Dangerous Fathers, Problem Mothers and Terrible Teens*. New York, 1958.

McCracken, Elizabeth. *The American Child*. New York, 1913.

Mead, Margaret. *Blackberry Winter*. New York, 1972.

———. *Culture and Commitment*. New York, 1970.

——— and Wolfenstein, Martha, eds. *Childhood in Contemporary Culture*. Chicago, 1955.

Melody, William. *Children's Television: The Economics of Exploitation*. New Haven, 1973.

Meyer, Ernest C. *Infant Mortality in New York City*. New York, 1921.

Miller, Daniel R., and Swanson, Guy E. *The Changing American Parent*. New York, 1958.

Mole, Dr. Albert. *The Sexual Life of the Child*. New York, 1929.

Neumann, Henry. *Modern Youth and Marriage*. New York, 1928.

Peck, Ellen. *The Baby Trap*. New York, 1971.

Platt, Anthony M. *The Child Savers*. Chicago, 1969.

Post, Emily. *Children Are People.* New York, 1940.

Radl, Shirley L. *Mother's Day Is Over.* New York, 1973.

Richmond, Winifred. *The Adolescent Girl.* New York, 1925.

Ritchie, Oscar W., and Koller, Marvin R. *Sociology of Childhood.* New York, 1964.

Robitscher, Jonas, ed. *Eugenic Sterilization.* Springfield, Ill., 1973.

Ross, Dorothy. *G. Stanley Hall.* Chicago, 1972.

Sadler, William. *Growing Out of Babyhood.* New York, 1940.

Salk, Lee. *What Every Child Would Like His Parents to Know.* New York, 1973.

Sangster, Margaret E. *From My Youth Up.* New York, 1909.

Seabury, Katherine. *The Fun of Having Children.* Boston, 1935.

Sears, Robert R.; Maccoby, Eleanor E.; and Levin, Harry. *Patterns of Child Rearing.* New York, 1957.

Spock, Benjamin. *Baby and Child Care.* New York, 1947.

———. *Problems of Parents.* Boston, 1962.

———. *Raising Children in a Difficult Time.* New York, 1974.

Strait, Suzanne. *Children and Their Parents.* Fremont, N.Y., 1968.

Strecker, Edward A., and Lathbury, Vincent T. *Their Mothers' Daughters.* New York, 1956.

Thompson, Ruth W. *Training My Babes.* Boston, 1929.

Tudor-Hart, Beatrix. *The Intelligent Parent's Guide to Child Behavior.* New York, 1966.

Watson, John B. *The Psychological Care of Infant and Child.* New York, 1928.

Weill, Blanche C. "Are You Training Your Child to Be Happy?" Washington, D.C., 1930. (Pamphlet)

Wolf, Anna W. M. *The Parents' Manual.* New York, 1962.

AUTHOR'S NOTE: Besides the above, I consulted pamphlets and magazine and newspaper articles too numerous to list. Among these, I found the pamphlets put out over the years by the Child Study Association of particular value; also "Sixty Years of Child Training Practices," by Celia B. Stendler (*Journal of Pediatrics*, January, 1950); "Early American Childhood in the Middle Atlantic States," by Sister Monica Kiefer (*Pennsylvania Magazine of History and Biography*, January, 1944); "Aristocracy in Colonial America," by Arthur Schlesinger (*Massachusetts Historical Society Proceedings*, 1961–62); and "Trends in Infant Care," by Martha Wolfenstein (*American Journal of Orthopsychiatry*, 1953).

Index